FINDING LIFE WITH GOD

5 KEYS TO THRIVING
THEO MYER

LIFE WITH GOD
RESOURCES

Life with God Resources

CONTENTS

Dedication

To my partner in life, love, and the enjoyment of God: Gayleen, you are God's greatest gift to me on this earth. All of the thoughts in this book come from our heart, our discussions, and our experiences (together and apart) with our Center and Brother, Jesus.

Acknowledgements

This book is the result of a community of so many people helping me. Thanks to my church communities at Corralitos Community Church and New Beginnings—I have learned so much from you. I had a wonderful group of people who gave input on this book, including Ariel Bauder-Klay, Ricky Bocanegra, Sierra Dermott, Gayleen Barnes Myer, Sallie Smith, and Dan Wilkins. Finally, Jennifer Twomley brought more style and clarity in her professional edit. I see you all and I'm grateful for each one of you!

INTRODUCTION

Growing up, my sports passions were football and basketball. As a middle-school student, I spent many lunch recesses playing football with a "ball" made of foil from the cafeteria lunches. With that two-inch piece of wadded tinfoil, we lined up and played two-hand touch

football (instead of tackle) for the rest of recess. Or, if we could find an inflated ball, we would shoot baskets in the hot sun and play six-on-six basketball. Mild violence due to losing was a common feature of these games. Someone on the losing football team would two-hand "touch" someone to the ground by shoving them onto the asphalt, or they would commit a "hard foul" that sent a driving basketball player sprawling (probably a little acting involved, TBH!). I spent many hours enjoying these sports, and I later played on school teams and in rec leagues.

Baseball was the ugly stepsister of these three sports for me. While I spent hundreds of hours playing basketball and football, I only played baseball when required in PE class. Still, when I was in my twenties and my church softball team needed players, I got recruited. Whenever we played a new team and I stepped up to bat, the outfielders would back away, because I looked like a guy who could hit with power. After one or two swings, they would come in a little. The next time I batted, the defense would stay put, and as the game wore on, it became clear to them that I was not a threat to hit a long bomb. I was a little frustrated to see them come in closer, expecting a short hit, but I rarely punished them for their low expectations.

I didn't understand why I couldn't hit that ball like some other people on my team. I had quick reflexes and a muscular build, but people who looked less athletic outplayed me in every game. Then one day someone gave me a suggestion: "Don't try to hit the ball hard. Try to swing the bat fast." That turned out to be a revelation to me, and my next hit flew over the heads of the outfielders. From then on, I was a much better batter, because I reminded myself each time I stepped up to bat: "Swing the bat fast."

That coaching unlocked a new level of success at softball. I had it in me, but I needed a key to unlock that success.

Practical, Possible, Powerful

In the story of my life, better softball skill ranks low on my list of accomplishments. Despite my progress, I have not had any offers from Major League Baseball teams . . . yet. But this pattern of unlocking new potential has repeated itself many times in my life in more important areas: my relationship with God, my marriage, parenting my kids, maintaining my health, becoming a more effective leader, and overcoming addictions. My life has been deeply changed, and I have found dramatic surges of joy, new levels of understanding who I am, and a deeper connection with God.

The most significant changes in my life have come through spiritual breakthroughs. Jesus seems to think that the GCTJ app (God-Connection-Through-Jesus) is the most important one to install on our "heart phone" (a device even more important than our smartphone!). He said this:

> *My purpose is to give them a rich and satisfying life.*
> John 10:10

In this book, I will use the phrase "Life with God" to mean the ideal rich and satisfying life that Jesus talks about in this verse. It's the kind of life that Jesus lived. Life with God is the abundant life lived in connection with God and His resources. Something exciting about Jesus' statement is that it tells us He wants to help us find Life with God! Life with God is colored by love, joy, peace, goodness, and meaningful impact. One of my passions is to help people unlock this type of abundant living. Too many of us live a black-and-white existence, because we can't find the color saturation slider God installs in our hearts. We live in black and white when there are deep orange sunsets and golden poppy flowers all around us. We are playing with a tinfoil ball instead of a real football. We are swinging our bats hard instead of fast. Jesus offers more!

When I worked as a high school teacher, something I learned was the importance of giving simple and complete instructions so everyone knew what to do. There was an unspoken deal in my classroom: if a student would truly listen and work hard, I would teach them how to ace the class. I needed to teach in a way that was practical and possible, leading to powerful, deep understanding. As a pastor, I have this same goal in helping others find Life with God—to offer people keys that are practical, possible, and powerful.

I want you to have the rich and satisfying life that Jesus intends for you—a thriving Life with God. If that's also what you want, I can help. I want to make significant growth easy for you, so I will be very specific and plain as I explain this life. I will approach Life with God from several different angles. What you will learn isn't anything new in the history of those who follow Jesus. Instead, I am packaging ancient truth into something new and easy to use. The lessons I share come from the Bible and from 2,000 years of people who have followed Jesus. I want to see supernatural power in your life, a thriving and honorable character, and fresh ways for God to use you to help and care for others.

Old Path—New App

When I hear people offer wisdom for how to follow Jesus, I am suspicious of new fads. When it comes to God's truth, I prefer to accept the weight of thousands of years of prayer and thought and Bible meditation by people filled with the Holy Spirit. Throughout history, I see a multitude of people whose lives and words show me they truly experienced and understood Life with God. People as varied as Saint Paul (first century), Augustine (fourth century), Teresa of Àvila (sixteenth century), and Richard Foster (twenty-first century) still speak through their works with familiarity and depth about Life with God. It's no coincidence that these heroes shared similar thoughts about the abundant, God-filled life.

As I said, the information in this book is not new. It is a new package of ancient ideas. It is an updated user interface for archived data. It is a balanced approach to Life with God, which has been tested in my life and the lives of many in our church community. It is a modern battery-powered tool to help you copy Jesus the carpenter's handiwork. The heart of this book is ancient, as old as Jesus Himself. The Apostle Paul (who I will call Pastor Paul in this book) lived at the same time Jesus did, and he passionately described Life with God as getting to know Jesus, having the power of Jesus' resurrection in his own life, and living out of sacrificial love for others.[1] (BTW, these little numbers are endnotes, and if you are interested in more information you can turn to them at the very back of the book and look for the number.)

My goal with the 5 Keys introduced in this book is to show you how to let God transform your heart so you reflect more of His goodness and love. Who was I thinking about as I wrote about Life with God?

- The 5 Keys are for new believers who have little or no church background. Reading this will give you practical information for a good, strong start in your faith.

- The 5 Keys are also for those who have followed Jesus for years but feel stalled in your walk with God. This book will show you the biblical principles and habits that jumpstart spiritual growth.

- The 5 Keys are for anyone who wants to help someone else find a joyful, rich Life with God. This tool tucks centuries of Holy Spirit-guided wisdom and Bible lessons into a simple handbook you can share with others.

How to Use This Book

Each of the 5 Keys answers a different question about Life with God.

Key 1: What is the first step in a Life with God?

Life with God begins with *a miracle*, when a person says "Yes" to Jesus as their Rescuer and Leader in life. We will talk about six things that change when someone chooses Jesus. Once this spiritual re-creation occurs, we can have a deep connection with God and new divine resources.

Key 2: What are the most important goals in a Life with God?

Jesus gives us *two missions* as His followers: the Great Commandments and the Great Commission. These callings give our lives direction and purpose as we channel God's love and goodness through our hearts into the lives of those we love.

Key 3: What should we focus on moment by moment in a Life with God?

In our moment by moment Life with God, *three motifs* (Yes, this is a strange word—I'll explain it later!) should play as a beautiful soundtrack to our lives. We can learn how to stay constantly connected with God through the Holy Spirit (this is called "abiding" in the Bible), how to be authentic with God and others, and how to enjoy the good things in life.

Key 4: What is the kind of love that comes from a Life with God?

There are *four measures* of love in Life with God that should be in balance, like a wheel with four spokes. Jesus' life overflowed with these four aspects of love: growing in relationship with God, caring for His followers in community, serving those outside His community, and sharing Jesus with those who haven't found Life with God yet.

Key 5: What are the regular habits that support a thriving Life with God?

Here we get down to a simple, doable plan for thriving in our Life with God. We can't jump straight here without the other four Keys, but this Key brings us *five methods* that make it practical. These five habits take about seven hours a week, and the results will allow God to become a deep influence and pivotal person in your life.

Each chapter will include questions for you to answer on your own or with others, as well as some extra resources if you want to dive deeper into that aspect of Life with God.

Before You Continue

One of the constant struggles in this life is our tendency to want to do things on our own. This is often rooted in being hurt or disappointed by others. The great news is that God is unlike anyone we have met in this world! With Him it's safe to set aside our natural hesitancy and independence. Completely trusting a God who knows us fully and loves us perfectly is actually a very wise step!

There is only One who can change us so deeply that we become a transformed person. He is our Father God. So, each time you open this book, ask our Good Father to read with you. Trust Him to lead you, help you, love you, and show you His truth. As you open this book, open your heart to God, and He will guide your thoughts and emotions as you read. You will see a small triangle pointing up (Δ) next to each chapter title to remind you to connect with our heavenly Father each time you read. I encourage you to say this simple prayer.

Δ Δ Δ Δ Δ Δ Δ Δ Δ Δ Δ Δ Δ Δ Δ Δ

Our Father, I hunger for more of You in my life, but I need Your help. Before I read, I open my heart to You and read with spiritual focus. Speak to me, God, and I will say "Yes."

Δ Δ Δ Δ Δ Δ Δ Δ Δ Δ Δ Δ Δ Δ Δ Δ

Questions to Help You Thrive

At the end of every chapter, you will find questions to help you grow. If you are reading this book with a group, these can help start a meaningful discussion. If you are reading on your own (Remember, God is reading with you!), the questions are for you and God to process together.

1. Do you feel that your life could be richer than it is now?

2. What do you think Jesus meant when He said, "My purpose is to give them a rich and satisfying life"?

3. Where are you struggling or unsatisfied in your life?

4. Which of the 5 Keys to Life with God sparks the most interest for you?

5. What part of this Introduction is still unclear?

MIRACLE

Life with God is a personal encounter with the Infinite Being who is completely good and present in all places and at all times. It shouldn't surprise us that the first big step toward Life with God is to allow God to upgrade us!

The Miracle Key explains how Life with God is catapulted to a new level when we first trust Jesus as our Rescuer and Leader. The Miracle Key graphic has a burst of light to indicate the explosion of new gifts given by God in that powerful moment: forgiveness, new identity, and new resources. These new spiritual abilities are given in an instant, but Life with God means we get to slowly master using these gifts for the rest of lives!

You might want to read about the Miracle Key if:

- You want to experience God in every moment of your life

- You are trying to live like Jesus through willpower alone

- You are unsure if you have been forgiven, filled with God's Spirit, or will spend eternity with God in heaven

MIRACLE Δ

THE STARTING POINT

By spiritual birth, I mean that great change
which God works in the soul
when he brings it from death to life;
when he awakens those who sleep in sin,
and gives them power to become the sons of God.
(John Wesley, 18th century)

This quote is from one of my spiritual heroes who lived in the 1700s, a man named John Wesley. Young John Wesley was religious. In fact, he was an ordained priest in the Church of England, and he served a local church in northern England. When Wesley was 32, he left on a missionary trip to a strange, foreign place in the New World called Georgia (yes, the US state

Georgia). After a few years of disappointing missionary work, he returned to England with a deep sense of falling short as a Christian. Then something happened that changed his life and faith. This is what John Wesley wrote in his journal to describe the change that happened in his heart:

> I went very unwillingly, to a small group in Aldersgate Street, where one was reading Martin Luther's preface to the Epistle of the Romans. About a quarter before nine, while he was describing the change that God works in the heart through faith, I felt my heart strangely warmed, and I believed for the first time. When I told my brother we sang a hymn with great joy.[2]

His brother, Charles Wesley, also trusted in Jesus for the first time that night, even though he had also lived a religious life. Both brothers realized that trying to follow Jesus' example was not enough. The only way to become a child of God was to accept forgiveness as a gift made

John Wesley

possible by Jesus dying in their place. They both had been trying to earn their salvation instead of just admitting their sin, accepting forgiveness, choosing to follow Jesus, and receiving the Holy Spirit. Charles Wesley wrote a song to describe his own miraculous heart change.

No condemnation now I dread
  Jesus, and all in him is mine,
Alive in him, my living head
  And clothed in righteousness, divine,
Bold I approach the Eternal Throne
  And claim my crown through Christ my own[3]

Until that powerful event at Aldersgate, John and Charles Wesley were not "in Christ," and Christ was not in them. They lived by good works and not by faith. But in the moment they first believed, a miracle happened, and God placed His Holy Spirit in them. Life with God starts with this miracle.

What Changes When I Become a Child of God?

Let's look at what the Bible says about the miracle of spiritual rebirth and its transforming results in us. John, the biographer of Jesus, said:

> *But to all who believed him [Jesus] and accepted him, he gave the right to become children of God. They are reborn—not with a physical birth resulting from human passion or plan, but a birth that comes from God.*
>
> John 1:12–13

Now, God loves everybody, so whether you're a follower of Jesus or not, God loves you. But the Bible tells us that those who accept and follow Jesus are given the special title of "children of God." A supernatural birth happens in our life when we trust in Jesus as our Rescuer and Leader, and this "birth that comes from God" is what makes us His children. What a special privilege and gift!

In general, relationships grow slowly over time, but sometimes there are big jumps that happen along the way. One of those big jumps in our relationship with God occurs when we realize that Jesus is truly the One. Although we've heard many people talk about how we should live, Jesus' words now resonate more deeply in our heart. We now know that He is the only One who loves us with an unselfish and sacrificial love. Jesus is the One sent by God to give us the truth that allows us to find God.

At the same time, we feel the impossibility of Jesus' high calling to love God and others completely. Compared to some people around us, we can feel like we're doing pretty well morally. I watch reality TV and think, "Dang, I'm pretty healthy compared to these wackos!" But when I compare myself to Jesus, I look bad. And it's not just Jesus who reveals how I fall short. When I compare myself to a person like Mother Teresa or Nelson Mandela, I don't measure up either. I definitely need a miracle to be like Jesus. I need God to install new hardware in my heart.

In the very moment when this "birth that comes from God" happens, the Bible describes many wonderful things that happen simultaneously. This miracle brings a burst of divine power that changes a person at the most foundational level. I wish I could tell you ALL the ways God changes us, but here are the six biggest changes you can expect when you trust in Jesus and become His follower.

Forgiveness

One generous gift God's spiritual birth gives us is forgiveness. When we choose Jesus as our Rescuer, God forgives all of the times we have lived selfishly and hurt others. We don't earn this forgiveness—we accept it as a gift from Jesus.[4] The "birth that comes from God" gives us an astonishing gift that cost Jesus His life. Being forgiven makes us so grateful! It also makes us willing to admit we struggle and need forgiveness often. Once we experience the miracle of forgiveness, we are transformed into people who are not crushed by making selfish, hurtful mistakes. We regret our mistakes but find release and freedom from shame through forgiveness.

Becoming a New Child of God

When this miracle occurs—you are adopted into God's family![5] You become a princess or prince of the King. God's kids are the brothers and sisters of the One who is the ruler of all: Jesus Christ. When the miracle of new life happens, you are united with the Spirit of God and marked as His child. It is the greatest upgrade in status possible, and a great privilege only possible because of the kindness (grace) of God. This is the core of my self-image—being God's child—and it is a high honor to be a child of the King! How cool is that!!!

The Holy Spirit in Us

Another benefit is that the Spirit of God makes a home inside of us. God's Holy Spirit comes and blends with our own spirit, and we become a miraculous mixture of human and divine.[6] This fundamentally changes who we are. What else happens when we receive the Holy Spirit? We now have a direct connection with God, and His Spirit begins to influence who we are. The Spirit speaks to us and says, "You are part of God's family, and I'll help you live that way!"

This means the Holy Spirit shows us what jobs God has set aside for us. It means we learn to relate to each other the way God relates to us. For example, we forgive people. If someone comes to me and says, "I am so sorry for what I've done," my response is to forgive them. That's part of what it means to be in God's family.

Constant Connection to God

When the miracle happens, you become connected to God because you have His Spirit in you.[7] Now when we read the Bible, the words of God not only flow into our mind but also into our heart. The Holy Spirit miraculously brings those words to life in your heart, so they're not just words on a page. We recognize that we're not reading a book but listening to wisdom from the One who loves us.

In the daily grind of your life, God is there with you. It's like having your best friend at your side, but that best friend is also the wisest and most caring person in the universe—God! Suddenly everything we do becomes an adventure shared with God, and the hard times are different because He is there with us . . . always. Constant connection is a joyful possibility in Life with God.

Heart Change

When you choose Jesus and receive His life, you'll experience heart change.[8] You know why? Because being with God changes us. Standing and worshiping God changes us. Letting His love pour through us as we read the Bible changes us. Allowing the Spirit to help us when we are overwhelmed changes us. The person I was forty years ago is not the person I am today, much to my delight. I'm more patient and compassionate, less prideful, and more aware of who I am. I'm excited for you to experience the miracle and begin the exciting journey of heart change.

Eternity with God in Heaven

The last change you can expect when you trust Jesus is the one that many Christians talk about the most: heaven.[9] You will be with God forever. His Holy Spirit comes to live inside of you, and when your body dies, the Spirit will guide your spirit right into God's presence. The Spirit guides us home, and we spend eternity with the same God we have learned to walk with in our earthly life. When we are constantly connected to Him in this world, it's no surprise that when we die, we go immediately to be with Him in heaven.

This is what life is really about: being connected to God. Jesus said:

> *And this is the way to have eternal life—to know you, the only true God, and Jesus Christ, the one you sent to earth.*
>
> John 17:3

Do you get what Jesus is saying? Eternal life is knowing God intimately. Heaven is the end result of this miracle of a life with God that begins right now, right here in this world. Your joyful Life with God will continue forever!

So HOW Do I Become a Child of God?

Short answer: say "Yes" to God when He asks if you accept Jesus. That means agreeing He is your source of truth and forgiveness and your example to follow in life. God is always looking for people at this place in their spiritual journey. This person comes to realize that Jesus is special, the One who makes a way for us to get to God. They realize that God loves them and wants to partner with them through this life. They accept that when their physical life is over, they will be with God because of the sacrifice of Jesus, not because they did so many good things or didn't do so many bad things. They will live forever because Jesus died for them.

Often this change of life direction happens in a memorable moment where a person chooses Jesus. Sometimes this "Yes" happens over time. I know people who knew they weren't a follower of Jesus three months ago, and now they are a follower of Jesus. Sometime in those three months it happened, but they don't know exactly when. At some point, maybe unknown to us, our heart responds to Jesus and we say, "This is my Shepherd. This is the One who's going to lead me. This is the One I'm going to follow even into the darkest valley. I'm living my life *for* this One and *with* this One."

When you take this step in your spiritual journey, the miracle happens. In some ways, it's a very simple process and easy to do. You could say "Yes" to Jesus right now. Some of you have been attending a church for years, but you might be like John Wesley. You might be living life in your own strength and still trying to work your way to God. The incredible news is that today you can simply accept a gift that changes everything!

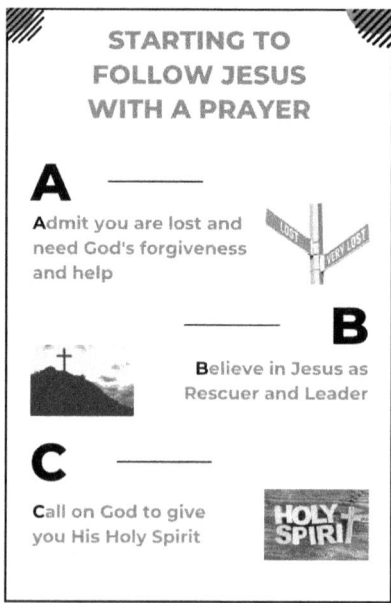

STARTING TO FOLLOW JESUS WITH A PRAYER

A ——
Admit you are lost and need God's forgiveness and help

—— **B**
Believe in Jesus as Rescuer and Leader

C ——
Call on God to give you His Holy Spirit

Making this choice is as easy as ABC but as serious as saying "I do" at your wedding ceremony.

Admit that you're lost and in need of God's forgiveness and direction. You need His help in life.

Believe in Jesus as your Rescuer and your Leader in life. You're ready to follow after Him and let Him guide you. And then you

Call on God to put his Holy Spirit inside of you.

This simple prayer from a sincere heart will change your life. It will allow you to live more like Jesus in a way you never could without God's Spirit in you.

Δ Δ Δ Δ Δ Δ Δ Δ Δ Δ Δ Δ Δ Δ Δ Δ

Dear God, I admit that I need you. I need your help, and I need your forgiveness for so many parts of my life. I believe in Jesus as the One who died to forgive me, and I need Him to be my guide. I choose to follow Jesus. Please put Your Holy Spirit inside of me to make me Your own child and connect me to You forever. Amen

Δ Δ Δ Δ Δ Δ Δ Δ Δ Δ Δ Δ Δ Δ Δ Δ

There was an old man who liked to split his own wood, though he would always go out and just use a sledgehammer and a maul, swinging away. His friends told him, "You've got to get a log splitter." Since he was getting a little bit older, he started to consider this. When he finally decided to do it, he went down to Home Depot, got a log splitter, and towed it home. A week later, he towed it back to Home Depot. "This thing is useless!" he said at the return counter. "I only split half as much wood as splitting by hand!" The worker stepped over to the log splitter and started the engine to see how it was working, and when it roared to life the man looked surprised and said, "Hey, what's that noise?"

And that's what it's like to try to live Life with God without the power of this miracle in your life. It's like trying to use a log splitter without starting the engine. All of us desperately need to get that power in our life, and once you do, it will change the way you can live!

So, Life with God starts with a miracle: that's our first Key.

Questions to Help You Thrive

1. Why does everyone need a miracle to be able to live like Jesus?

2. Of the six aspects of this miracle (forgiveness, the Holy Spirit in us, becoming a new child of God, constant connection to God, heart change, and eternity with God in heaven), which is the most exciting to you?

3. If you are not ready to make the decision to follow Christ, can you explain what is blocking your way to Jesus?

4. How does a person know if they have become a child of

God?

5. If you have experienced this miracle, describe some of the differences before and after you became God's kid.

Resources for a Deeper Dive

For a practical approach to exploring what it means to follow Jesus
- *Finding Your Way Back to God*, by Dave and Jon Ferguson

If you're sorting through objections to faith
- *Confronting Christianity*, by Rebecca McLaughlin

Missions

Simplify. This is a big part of what a good teacher does for students. Simplifying can be dangerous, because too much can be lost when we trim and focus on a few things instead of many. That's why only the best teachers can do it well.

The Missions Key is about simplifying our focus. And there is good news! Jesus is the master teacher who simplified our mission perfectly. He gave us two "great" missions: the Great Commandments and the Great Commission. Our Missions Key graphic has a heart on it to remind us that love is the center of Life with God.

You might want to read about the Missions Key if:

- You have trouble focusing on a lot of details and want a simple version of Jesus' teachings

- You are a big-picture thinker who likes to connect daily decisions with big goals

- You feel overwhelmed by the big ways your character and actions need to change to be like Jesus

MISSION: GREAT COMMANDMENTS Δ

The clarity and perception of truth and wisdom
makes a person see that everyone is made for love,
which God wraps forever around His own.
(Julian of Norwich, 14th century)

The second of the Keys to Life with God is the missions Jesus has given to us. Having the big picture—the big goals—spelled out for us is so helpful! Plus, we all need purpose in this life. We need to serve something bigger than ourselves. If we're simply living life for ourselves, there's just a good deal of emptiness to it. Jesus knows that you and I and all of His followers need an important mission, and He has given us two great ones!

I'm probably about twenty years away from not being on this planet anymore. I find myself thinking about how I spend my time as I get older, because I want to have done something that is meaningful in my life. I've been a high school teacher, and I've been a pastor, and I've accomplished some things I'm proud of in my life. But I want to be sure I'm doing the best things. That means doing what God thinks is best. So, we human beings need some clarity in our purpose, and Jesus provides us with two key missions, which guide us into joyful Life with God.

We will talk about these two great missions in the next two chapters. I use the word "great" on purpose because followers of Jesus for centuries have used the word "great" to name these two missions from Jesus. We'll talk about the Great Commandments in this chapter and the Great Commission in our next chapter. These missions add to our Life with God.

What is the First Mission from God?

The first mission Jesus gives us is the Great Commandments. When Jesus was asked "What is the focus of life?" or "How can you sum up everything in one little sentence?" here is the answer the master teacher Jesus gave:

> *"You must love the LORD your God with all your heart, all your soul, all your strength, all your mind."*
>
> Luke 10:27

Jesus says that we should love God first and love Him with everything we've got. Give God everything—all your time, talent, and treasure. Listen to Him, and if His opinion is different from someone else's, don't listen to them! The goal is to be devoted to Jesus with every thought and resource you have. This is a difficult mission, which I rarely achieve in practice. Jesus calls us to a focus and a hunger for God that is unique in our life. Passion for more of Him should be greater than our desire for anything or anyone else.

This relationship with God redefines our understanding of love. We learn to love as we interact with God, and God's love fills us and changes us so we can love Him, ourselves, and others in that same way. Jesus goes on to say:

> *"You must love the LORD your God with all your heart,*
> *all your soul, all your strength, and all your mind."*
> **And "Love your neighbor as yourself."**
>
> Luke 10:27

First, we throw ourselves into loving God and learn what real love is. Then we love God, ourselves, and others with this same love.[10] Our mission in the Great Commandments is to let our hunger to know God lead us into a deep relationship with Him that fills us up, and then to have that same love in our life. People who love while having a deep relationship with God are able to love others better.

Julian of Norwich wrote beautifully about the importance of love, and I included her words at the start of this chapter: ". . . everyone is made for love, which God wraps forever around his own." Isn't that beautiful? All of us are made for love, which God wraps around us

Julian of Norwich

like a cloak. We can't be the people we are meant to be until God's love wraps around us, because only His love satisfies the deep need for love that we all have. Once we have a full serving of love, we can share pure love with other people. Our needs are met, so we can be more selfless, we can be more sacrificial, we can be more kind, and we can be more gracious to people, even when it's difficult.

Julian of Norwich is famous for her love of cats. Now, in my experience, cats are usually independent and distant creatures who only let you pet them when they need a scratch. Someone who is filled with God's love can happily have a cat as a pet, overcoming that snooty attitude which says "You are not worthy!" (Here's an insider tip from me, a dog person: get a dog and know devoted love!)

What is the Second Mission from God?

A picture in the Bible tells us how we love others after we get to know God and His love.[11] God's love is a fountain that flows into us and fills us up with His love. The Bible says that we love because He first shows us what love is. Our first step is to experience God's love deeply. When His Spirit lives inside us, He bathes our heart with God's love.

You may feel God's love when you see a small blessing that God gives you in your day or as you sing worship songs at your church. God's love may become real when you are walking in nature or as you read your Bible. You suddenly notice He is with you, and love fills you. In that moment, you may experience and recognize the absurd fact that God loves you—not everybody, but you! He made you just the way He wanted to, and He enjoys your personality. There are times when God is proud of you for the way you are reflecting His love and goodness. But even when you're messing up, He still loves you. His amazing love pours into all of us, and it fills us up, and it helps us love Him better. It helps us love ourselves better. In time, it naturally overflows to loving others better too.

This is the process of having overflowing love for others. So be hungry for God's love, and let His love fill you up! Don't expect your spouse or your family to do this, because only God is big enough to give you the love you need. Then overflow will naturally happen. You will begin to be more kind and patient and faithful because He is. And then loving is not something we are pretending to do—we love genuinely, enjoying people and helping them sacrificially and sticking with them through ups and downs.

So, the first mission Jesus gives us is loving God and then loving Him, ourselves, and others out of the overflow. The next mission is also about love—about loving others in a way that is at the core of God's heart.

Questions to Help You Thrive

1. Is it exciting to you that love is at the center of God's universe?

2. How would your life change if you felt "wrapped in God's love" all the time?

3. What would change in your life if everything you did was seen as an act of love?

4. Do you have an example in your life of a time when God

helped you to love someone who was difficult to love when you first met them?

5. When do you feel God's love the most?

Resources for a Deeper Dive

Experiencing God's love more
- *Abba's Child,* by Brennan Manning

Overcoming a performance orientation
- *You are Special,* by Max Lucado (children's book, but profound)

Loving Others
- *Love Does,* by Bob Goff

MISSION: GREAT COMMISSION Δ

When the Lord ascended into heaven, He did not leave us,
but came to us. For He said, 'And be sure of this:
I am with you always, even to the end of the age.'
He is with us, not only by His divinity,
but by His grace, by His power, by His truth.
And therefore, the very command that He gave to His
disciples, to go and preach the Gospel to all nations, is a
command for all of us who are His disciples.
(Augustine of Hippo, 4th century)

You might be surprised that the first great mission God gives us is loving Him, ourselves, and others. Not a big list of dos and don'ts, but love! He wants us to be known for love. He said people will know we're Jesus' followers because of our love for each other.[12]

The second great mission that God gives us is called the Great Commission. See how it has the word mission in it? Great Com-MISSION! This mission is one of Jesus' last messages to His followers. To put this command into context, Jesus had been horribly tortured and executed, and three days later He came back to life. When He was resurrected, He talked with His astounded followers. Can you imagine how much impact the words the risen Jesus spoke had on his followers?! During that time Jesus told them this:

> *Therefore, go and make disciples of all the nations,*
> *baptizing them in the name of the Father and the Son*
> *and the Holy Spirit. Teach these new disciples to obey*
> *all the commands I have given you.*
>
> Matthew 28:19–20

What Do "Disciple" and "Baptize" Mean?

Here we run into our first encounter with the fact that the Bible was written a long time ago to people who lived in a different culture than we do. Incredibly, we understand so much of the Bible when we read it, but we sometimes encounter things that are strange to us, especially in the Old Testament (Genesis through Malachi in our Bible).

A **disciple** in Jesus' time was a person who was a devoted follower of a religious or philosophical teacher. Famous teachers like Socrates and Plato had disciples. Among the Jewish people, young men who wanted to become teachers would choose a rabbi and then ask to be an apprentice who learned from the rabbi. Once accepted by a rabbi, that person would be immersed in water to symbolize a new birth as a disciple of a certain rabbi. Jesus' followers were also baptized, and Jesus welcomed both men and women as His disciples. The act of being dunked in water was called **baptism**, and people today are still baptized when they choose to follow Jesus.

Today a devoted follower on social media is someone who's always checking the social media of a certain person they admire. As soon as the celebrity posts something, their follower "likes it" or "loves it" with a heart emoji or a little comment like, "Oh, this is so beautiful!" I follow extreme sports, and my comments are more like, "You're insane and have a death wish!" As followers of Jesus, we should respond to His words too.

> Go and make disciples, baptizing them and teaching them about Life with God!

> Sure! That sounds like a great idea. I know lots of people who need You. I'll need Your help, Jesus, but I'm on it!

The same idea of "following" is true for us as disciples of Jesus. We read what He writes in the Bible. We listen to the Holy Spirit.

We're devoted. We're responding with "Yes" as much as we can. A disciple is a devoted, committed follower of Jesus.

What is the Third Mission from God?

So "making disciples" just means that God wants us to help others find Life with God. You see, God is passionate about rescuing people from their own bad tendencies. We were designed to have God's Spirit in us. God loves every person, created them uniquely, and came to rescue them from themselves through Jesus, His Son.

Jesus gave an image through a story to help us feel how much God wants people to reconnect with Him. Jesus pictures God as a gentle father who allows his son to take his inheritance and leave his house. Then the son experiences serious problems and failures and realizes life is better back home. When the son returns home, ashamed and sorry for his offensive request, the father has been waiting for him with a heavy heart. When he sees his son, the father rejoices, wraps his arms around him, and throws a party.[13]

God the Father, who created every person, is waiting with a heavy heart for every person to come home to Him. I watch many parents grieve when their teen or adult child is taking a dark path, just as the son did in this story Jesus told. It might be drugs or homelessness or mental health issues that are untreated, or perhaps a person in their life who is influencing them to make destructive choices. A parent whose child is in danger struggles to be at peace until their child is safe.

So God, the perfect parent, does not want anyone to live without His love and resources, and God does not want anyone to die and spend eternity apart from Him in a place without love or kindness or anything good.[14] That place is called hell, and we get a taste of hell here on earth sometimes when sadistic dictators enjoy hurting others. God wants to protect those He loves from eternal death.

Knowing that God feels passionate about saving people, we want to help others find Life with God. Loving God means caring for those He cares for!

How Does Sharing Our Faith Show We Love Others?

I remember very clearly the moment I finally understood that helping others find Life with God was part of loving them, not some separate mission. When that happened, my approach to the Great Commission changed radically.

As a college student I was part of a group that would go to nearby colleges and try to get students to become followers of Jesus. This always seemed awkward to me, as we would descend on the cafeteria or open courtyards and look for people who were alone. Then we would ask them a question: "If you died tonight, are you sure you would go to heaven?"

I wanted to fulfill this Great Commission from God, so I went to share Jesus each week, even though it felt strange. I didn't see sharing the Gospel (the Bible calls the Good News about Life with God the "Gospel") as earning me some spiritual reward, but I did want to obey Jesus. In all the evenings I visited these campuses, I didn't see one person choose Jesus. What I did experience was lots of arguing with other students about religious ideas. Even when I clearly "won" the argument (or thought I did), people didn't choose Jesus. I felt defeated week after week, and as an introvert I dreaded those nights and felt exhausted afterwards.

A few years later, I was spending time with God in prayer, and I was reading the Great Commandments. I had one of those moments when a new and powerful thought pops into your head. Now I recognize that's how the Holy Spirit works sometimes: it was an encounter with God! I was supposed to love others by caring for them and being generous with them and serving them—AND as one expression of that love I was called to help them find Life with God. Now THAT was different from sharing Jesus out of obligation to God!

When I really loved someone, I naturally wanted them to discover Life with God. I sincerely wanted them to have the power of God's Spirit in their life. I truly wanted them to know forgiveness. I desperately wanted them to be with God for eternity. Suddenly it made sense: when you love someone, you want them to find Life with God too!

We have a funny saying in our church community: **Only share your faith with people you love.** If you don't love them, you won't do it right. We help others find Life with God because we want the best for them in this life and in the unending life that follows our physical death. It is an act of love for them *and* God. This love is the true motivation for the Great Com-MISSION.

How Do I Make Disciples?

To be really clear, it's not you or I who makes disciples. That's the work of God's Spirit once they say "Yes" to God. Still, we must have some part, since Jesus gave us this mission.

> *But you will receive power when the Holy Spirit comes upon you. And you will be my witnesses, telling people about me everywhere—in Jerusalem, throughout Judea, in Samaria, and to the ends of the earth.*
>
> Acts 1:8

Our part in the Great Com-MISSION, at its core, is to be witnesses—to simply tell the story of how God is working in our lives. That's what we share with those we love, and they're interested because they love us too. We talk about how God is helping us grow, overcoming anxiety and fear and selfishness; teaching us principles that are making our relationships work better; and changing our fear of death into a joyful expectation of a more intimate closeness with our dear Father God in heaven. This is our part in the work to call people home to the heart of the perfect parent, God. I will share more practical tips for you in the chapter about Key 5: Sharing Life List.

SUM (KEY 2 MISSIONS)

Missions are the big goals set by Jesus.

The **Great Commandments** call us to love God, ourselves, and others with Jesus' love.

The **Great Commission** reminds us to love people by helping them find Life with God.

Now I have shared with you about two of our five Keys. Key 1 is a miracle—the miracle that kickstarts Life with God. It's the miracle of a spiritual birth, the miracle of the Holy Spirit inside of us, and the miracle of becoming God's adopted child! Key 2 is the exciting missions Jesus invites us to carry out with His help. The first mission is the priority of love. The second mission is helping others find Life with God. What an inspiring, significant way to spend our life!

Questions to Help You Thrive

1. How do you feel about having two missions from God? Excited, overwhelmed, significant?

2. If you were sharing a God-story from your life and someone got offended and asked, "Why are you preaching at me?"—what would you say?

3. Jesus gives four commands in Matthew 28:19–20. The main one is "make disciples," but what are the other three?

4. How does helping others find Life with God show your love for God?

5. Do you feel natural sharing what God is doing in your life with people you love? What are the barriers you might need to overcome?

Resources for a Deeper Dive

- *Sharing Jesus Without Freaking Out,* by Alvin L. Reid

- *Getting Beyond "How Are You?",* by David Mains and Melissa Mains Timberlake

MOTIFS

*H*ow we do things is so important. When we share constructive criticism with a friend, *how* we do it is crucial to the success of our feedback. Our future friendship might hang on *how!* The Motifs Key is about *how* we live our lives.

A motif is a recurring theme, and in a movie, we find motifs in the soundtrack. When a villain appears, a dark or eerie theme plays. When the hero is interacting with her friends, we hear the energetic beat of modern pop music. These motifs convey who these characters are.

Our Motifs Key graphic has music notes to remind us of background music. Life with God has motifs too—the music of our life. No matter what activity we are doing, we can abide, be real, and enjoy the blessings in life.

You might want to read about the Motifs Key if:

- You wonder how being a follower of Jesus would affect your daily life

- You like to focus on the process more than the end goals

- You rarely hear from others that God shines through you

Motif: Abiding Δ

There are two natures in the believer, and so two ways of seeking holiness, as we allow the principles of the one or the other to guide us. The one is the carnal way, where we make our own efforts and resolutions, trusting Christ to help us as we struggle. The other is the spiritual way, where as those who have done and can do nothing, our one care is to receive Christ day by day and at every step to let Him live and work in us.

(Andrew Murray, 19th century)

Early in my spiritual journey, I came across the word *abide* in the Bible, and it seemed like a very important word. The problem was, I had never used the word *abide* in my whole life and had no idea what it meant. I tried reading books about abiding, but they were all filled with religious language that didn't help me much. I was frustrated and eventually paused my attempts to understand abiding.

What is Abiding?

Abiding sure seemed important when Jesus talked about Life with God. Listen to what He says:

> *Remain [abide] in me, and I will remain [abide] in you. For a branch cannot produce fruit if it is severed from the vine, and you cannot be fruitful unless you remain [abide] in me. Yes, I am the vine; you are the branches. Those who remain [abide] in me, and I in them, will produce much fruit. For apart from me you can do nothing.*
>
> John 15:4–5

The key to having the fruit of the Spirit[15] in our lives—love, joy, peace, patience, kindness, goodness, gentleness, self-control—is abiding. Jesus says that if I don't abide, I can "do nothing." Over the years, God has helped me understand abiding better, and I want to share what I learned so you can begin living this way much sooner than I did on my faith journey.

This word *abiding* means "staying connected." I want to give you some examples from the Bible so you can get a feel for how the word is used and how it works for a follower of Jesus.

The Bible says that we should abide in Jesus like a branch abides in a vine. Now let's put our definition in that sentence: we should stay connected to Jesus like a branch stays connected to the vine. OK, that makes a lot of sense. A branch needs to stay connected to the vine if it's  going to produce grapes. Cut it off from the vine, and it dies, producing nothing.

The Bible also says that God is love, and that if we abide in love, we will abide in God.[16] Now, when I hear that sentence, my brain just gets all mushy, because I don't know what the word *abide* means. But watch this: God is love, and if we "stay connected" to love, then we "stay connected" to God. Oh, wow! That's super meaningful, and I get it!

Let me give you one more example to help explain what abiding is. The Bible says that a person who does not love abides in death.[17] Just like before, when I hear that sentence, I don't really know what it means at first. So, let's put in our definition: a person who does not love stays connected to death. OK, so this means that people who do not have God's love in their heart are staying connected to death. Now that's a big deal! When we are connected to death, it is pouring darkness into our lives. That's a no bueno situation and something we would all want to avoid. I know the word *abiding* is unfamiliar, but I'm claiming it for followers of Jesus. It's a really important idea, and we need a word for it. If you want to know a little more about the word *abide* in the Bible, I explain it more in this endnote.[18]

How Does Abiding with God Affect Us?

Now let's go back and add our new definition to Jesus' words. By the way, did you know John was one of Jesus' closest friends? He listened closely to Jesus' words and passed them on to us.

> *"**Stay connected** to me, and I will **stay connected** to you. For a branch cannot produce fruit if it is severed from the vine, and you cannot be fruitful unless you **stay connected** to me. Yes, I am the vine; you are the branches. Those who **stay connected** to me, and I to them, will produce much fruit. For apart from me you can do nothing.*
>
> John 15:4–5

Our lives will show it if we are staying connected to Jesus. This is not a surprising statement, because we are affected by the people in our lives. Your brothers or sisters, your parents, your kids, your spouse—these people dramatically affect you. If you want to be affected by God, you have to stay connected to God in the same way. Jesus says that when we abide, we will produce the fruit of godly character and be more like Him.

By the way, since Jesus encourages us to abide in Him (stay connected to Him), that means it's also possible to disconnect from Him. It's possible to live our life, even after the miracle of new spiritual birth, disconnected from Him. Sadly, many people live this way! They are not abiding, not staying connected to God, and they live a somewhat barren life as a result. Instead of experiencing the fruit of God's Spirit, they experience extra pain and loneliness, and they miss opportunities to help others because they are not abiding. This is not how God meant for His kids to live. He wants rich spiritual fruit to grow in your life!

What is a Simple Description of How to Abide in Jesus?

I couldn't find a clear description of *abiding* when I was young in my faith. I'm going to try my best to do just that. I will try to explain it first with words, and then I'll use a picture to explain it in a different way. I'm praying God will help this beautiful truth come alive for you!

When I think of being connected to Jesus, I often think of those times when I'm singing worship songs with our church, praying during my Spiritual Boost time, or listening to God's voice in the Bible. In these times, I am only focused on God and nothing else. Abiding doesn't require this type of single focus. Abiding is being connected to Jesus like an app running in the background of my soul while I'm doing other things—an app that plays songs of God's love, presence, and resources. When I'm abiding, I'm living in partnership with God, asking Him for guidance and help as I need it. I'm anchored by His presence while I am doing other things.

Abiding changes my daily experience. There is a difference, I have learned, between eating and eating while abiding. There is a difference between talking with others and talking while abiding.

When I'm abiding, I recognize God moving in events that seemed random before. I react better to difficulties, because I have a sense of God's involvement and care in the challenges. I have access to His power to be more compassionate, more aware of the spiritual dynamics and the hearts of others, and more sensitive to how He might want to work through me. There's an open door between God and me, we're connected, and I'm following His lead. That's what I hope for you, and that's what Jesus intends for all of His followers.

The Cabin of My Heart

Since I was a teen, I have had an image that captures the place of my deepest, truest self. At my core, I see a cozy room in a cabin in the deep woods. This rustic room with a fire crackling is my soul, the place where I gather input from my mind, my emotions, and outsiders, and where I make choices minute by minute. Apparently, my true self likes 1950s furniture, but let's try to move on from my soul's outdated fashion trends!

The cabin in this picture shows my life when I'm not abiding with Jesus. At those times, I'm living my life with my own resources and gifts and doing the best that I can. I'm usually trying to follow the principles Jesus taught, and I can even be helping others in my own strength. It's a beautiful little cabin, and I work hard to keep it clean. At other times, especially when I'm overwhelmed, I'm not even aware that I'm making decisions—I'm just reacting. But this room is the control center for my life.

Thirty years ago I began to understand that God wanted to be with me in this room. I can stay connected to God in my soul. I can abide. The truth is, I'm still not great at staying connected to Him all the time. It's easy for me to do in spurts, but very hard for me to do constantly. It's a spiritual battle to abide, with dark spiritual forces fighting to distract me and separate me from God. Dark forces will fight against you, too, but Jesus will help you abide.

When I am abiding with God, a door opens in my room, and God floods into me. My cabin lights up! It may sound strange, but my normal, everyday life is suddenly filled with light. God is in the middle of it all—with me, for me, and working through me. There are supernatural resources. It's easier to love people. I'm more honest. I'm more compassionate with people. My ordinary life becomes a divine partnership, because God is walking with me in the most trivial parts of my life.

My struggle at abiding is a gift from God, because I realize that I can't do even this on my own.[19] I am forced to hope in God's transformation of my heart to grow in abiding. In the opening quote for this chapter by Andrew Murray, he talks about realizing that his own effort is not enough, that just trying harder is the "carnal" or ungodly way of life. The way of Jesus is to let God continually remake us and rely each moment on His power and presence. As I surrender, God's power flows and I abide more.

Can You Give Another Example of Abiding?

I am not alone in discovering the joy of abiding. Many other followers of Jesus have found the joy and power of staying connected to God. One of them was Frank Laubach. Frank lived in the early 1900s, and when he lost his dream job, he decided to go to the Philippines to teach English there. Once in his new country where people spoke a language he didn't understand, he wrote letters to his sons about opening his heart to God in a new way. He wrote to them about abiding, because Frank was trying to learn how to live a life connected to God all the time.

> For the past few days, I've been experimenting in a more complete surrender than ever before. I am taking by deliberate act of will, enough time from each hour to give God much thought. We used to sing a song in the church of my boyhood, which I liked, but which I never really practiced until now.

It says—
Moment by moment, I'm kept in his love.
Moment by moment, I have life from above,
Looking to Jesus, to glory, to shine,
Moment by moment, O Lord, I am Thine.

And it is exactly that, moment by moment, every waking moment, surrender, responsiveness, obedience, sensitiveness, pliability, lost in his love that I now have the mind bent to explore with all my might, it means two burning passions, first to be like Jesus, second to respond to God as a violin responds to the bow of the Master.[20]

Frank Laubach was on a spiritual journey to stay connected to God and His resources, and sometimes he succeeded and other times he failed. But when he did abide, it was so much better! And neither Frank nor I have any special personality trait that allows this deep connection. Jesus says it is the music that can play in every heart of those who follow Him. That means you can have your daily life transformed by God's presence!

If all of us as Jesus' followers can just abide a little bit more each day, we will truly be changed. There are times when I go a day or two without seriously thinking about God in my life, even recently—and I'm a pastor! I'm embarrassed to admit that, and it's crazy, because when I DO abide in God, my life is more joyful. Abiding in God is steadying. If all of us who are God's kids can let our weakness be overcome by relying on God, it will make a huge difference in our lives and in our world. That's your Father's beautiful intention for you—a life of abiding that brings rich joy and spiritual fruit to your heart and to others.

Questions to Help You Thrive

1. How would you define this word *abide?*

2. Read John 15:1–5. How does a branch abide in a vine?

3. How would you describe your feelings when God is close?

4. What are the things that distract you and make it hard to be aware of God's presence?

5. Do you know anyone who is an example of abiding? What do you notice about their life?

Resources for a Deeper Dive

- *The Practice of the Presence of God*, by Brother Lawrence

- *Letters by a Modern Mystic,* by Frank C. Laubach

MOTIF: BEING REAL Δ

> Be who God meant you to be,
> and you will set the world on fire.
> (Catherine of Siena, 14th century)

In living Life with God, the first motif is abiding. Staying connected to God should be the background music in our life—being aware of Him and relying on His resources. The second motif that should characterize our life when we follow Jesus is being honest—God wants you to be an authentic person. Telling the truth, though, is the enemy of denial. Followers of Jesus risk being honest with ourselves, we risk being transparent to trusted others, and we risk being truthful with God in prayer. We take a chance by letting others who are not followers of Jesus hear and see how God is working in us. Despite the danger of exposure, the truth is powerful. It is the starting point for real growth, and it will set you free to live the joyful, rich life God intends for you.

What Does It Mean to be Honest with God?

Abiding in God is the foundation we need so we can take off our masks. We become honest about who we are. We become honest about where we struggle. We become honest about where we are gifted and where we are weak. We are transparent. We are real. We are authentic.

Now, being honest will require a certain amount of security in your life. If you're worried about what other people think, or if you're trying to impress others, you will find it hard to be vulnerable. But I have good news for you! Our Father God will help you with this! As your needs for love, approval, and identity are met in your relationship with God, you will become more steady and less dependent on the affirmation of others. Anchored in God, you can find strength to be authentic.

One important tool to help build an authentic relationship with God is a commitment to honest prayer.

> *O my people, trust in him at all times. Pour out your heart to him, for God is our refuge.*
>
> Psalm 62:8

Sometimes as we learn to pray, we use words from others or from the Bible. Whether these words express our heart or not, we pray them because they sound good. We might feel uncomfortable saying hard things to God, so we stick with prayer that is from someone else's heart, not ours. Our personal prayers might become a recital of scripts we've used in public. Our doubts, our failures, and our feelings become out-of-bounds for talking to God, because we don't usually hear others pray this way in public. This is where the book of Psalms in the Bible helps us, because the songs included there often express doubts, fears, and negative feelings.

A real relationship with God means we pour out our hearts to Him, confident that He already knows us through and through, and that He loves us and can help us. We open ourselves to His love and truth in our hearts, believing that His transforming power can truly change us. You can tell God what is on your heart in prayer throughout your day. I know from experience this closeness with God enables us to be authentic with other people.

At one time in my own Life with God, I realized my prayers were often about what I read in the Bible that day instead of what I was struggling with in my life. There was this disconnect between my struggles and my relationship with God that put distance between God and me. So, I made a practical change in my daily time with God—I started that time by thinking about what had been on my heart and mind for the past day. Whatever that was, I talked about it with God. When I did that, I found God rejoiced and healed and helped and guided and confronted me. Being real with God brought me much closer to Him.

How Can I Be More Authentic with Myself?

To have a growing Life with God, our Father also invites us to be truthful with ourselves. Have you ever known someone who is always defensive when given constructive feedback? Often this means the defensive person is living with some unrealistic picture of themselves. They see themselves as a great friend, so they aren't open to feedback that could help them be a better friend. The Bible says that every person is capable of both darkness and light—darkness because we tend to live life our own way, and light because we bear the image of God and can reflect His goodness. Do you see how holding ourselves to a standard of perfection denies what the Bible says about who we are? Our Father knows you are not going to be perfect in this life. It's not admirable to expect perfection from ourselves—it's ungodly.

The swimmer was THIS big!

I have had to wrestle with my own dark places and accept God's help. Like I tend to make stories better than they were in real life when I retell them. My GPA goes up, the team I played (and won) against later went on to play professionally, and I'm pretty sure I saved the planet Earth from complete destruction . . . a few times. As a pastor, I have opportunities to lie each week in front of many people, so I need to get God's help to tell the less flashy, true story. He is the Hero, not me. God has challenged me to undershoot my contributions instead. It's good for my soul.

I encourage you to be a person who is aware of your weaknesses and not afraid to reveal them. In an honest Life with God, you can be someone who easily asks forgiveness for your mistakes. We should all be able to see our shortcomings because we know they're there, they can be forgiven, and God loves us in spite of them!

What About with Other Followers of Jesus?

Christians should be people with no masks, but too often we do a really bad job of living this way. Sometimes, in a church community, we try to put on these masks of being perfect people. This short-circuits the Holy Spirit's work in the group. What we really need is to be honest about all areas, even where we are not doing well. This encourages others to be honest about their struggles too. When we accept our limitations and faults, God can help us chart the path forward together. True community requires authentic relationships!

So, I encourage you to take off your mask. Listen to God call His church community to authenticity:

> *Don't just pretend to love others. Really love them. . . .*
> *Confess your sins to each other and pray for each other*
> *so that you may be healed.*
>
> Romans 12:9–10, James 5:16

I hope you will notice that I'm honest about my failures and weaknesses too. In this book and when I teach, I'm committed to transparency and hope it becomes a motif of our church community. I pray that our church will be a place where we don't only talk about our victories, but also about our failures. Where we admit our struggles to each other and pray so we might be healed. That's what these verses from the Bible are telling us—transparency should be the norm. This commitment to honesty will show others that we love people even when we know their struggles. When you are loved in a church community where you risk being known, you can begin to taste the unconditional love of God in that group. Once you feel loved for who you are, so much more is possible in your life! The motif of being real is a freeing part of Life with God.

What About Transparency with Those Who Need Jesus?

God invites us as His children to be changed deeply and then simply to be honest with the people around us so that they can see His transforming work in our hearts. That's all. That's His plan for reaching others. His plan is to change us so radically that other people notice it. People will instinctively know that these deep changes are not humanly possible, so it will reveal the power of God to them! I'll explain more about sharing with those who need Jesus in future chapters. For now, you can begin asking God to help you be honest about your life, no matter where you are in your faith journey with Him. If you wait until you have everything together before sharing with others, you will probably never share your faith!

What Are the Benefits of Being Real?

Being real pays off in many areas of our life. It helps us be humble. It encourages genuine community. It allows others to see real life change from God. And in our church, that kind of authenticity is what helped me know I wanted to commit to Corralitos Community Church, fondly called CCC.

I attended our church for eleven years before I became one of the pastors. How the Myer family chose this church community had to do with how real the people were. When we moved to the area, we were visiting various local churches and returned for a second visit to check out CCC. During the worship service, two people began to play a hymn called "In the Garden." The son played the banjo, while his dad sang and played the harmonica. When they got to the chorus of the song, the father sang:

> He walks with me,
> and He talks with me,
> and He tells me, I am His
> own.
> And the joy we share
> As we tarry there,
> None other has ever known.

And as he was singing these tender words about walking with Jesus, he started to cry.

As you might imagine, the worship center got very quiet. I wondered how the people were going to respond. Somebody said, "It's all right, Weese. We're with you."

Weese took a minute and pulled himself together, and then he said, "You know, this is my wife's favorite hymn. She's home right now, and she's sick with cancer. And she is having no trouble having faith in God, but I'm really having a hard time." Tears were running down his cheeks. After another minute of silence, he continued, "You know, I'm going to try to sing this song again. I'm going to have to sing it as a prayer, because this is not where I'm at—but this is where I wish I was." And he started to sing again.

I knew at that moment that this church community was the place for me and my family. That is the kind of community I want to be part of, where people can be real about what they're going through—a place where we can let God work on us, and no one's wearing an "I'm-fine" mask. I encourage you to be a part of a church community where most people talk about what's really happening in their lives. We all need that kind of place, that kind of authenticity, that kind of community where people risk being real.

Questions to Help You Thrive

1. What is the hardest thing for you about being real with God, yourself, and others?

2. Do you pray honestly most of the time or are you trapped by religious patterns when you talk with God?

3. How easy is it for you to get feedback from others about how they see you?

4. What prevents you from sharing honestly about what God is doing in your life?

5. How can you take one step toward more transparency in your life?

Resources for a Deeper Dive

- *Daring Greatly*, by Brené Brown (not a Christian book, but helpful)

- *God-Soaked Life*, by Chris Webb (section on "Fearless Honesty")

- *Confessions*, by Augustine of Hippo

MOTIF: ENJOYING △

> The heart overflows with gladness,
> and leaps and dances for the joy it has found in God.
> In this experience the Holy Spirit is active,
> and has taught us in the flash of a moment
> the deep secret of joy. You will have as much joy
> and laughter in life as you have faith in God.
> (Martin Luther, 16th century)

D ear friend, God has given us anytime access to abiding in Jesus, staying connected to Him moment by moment. This safe place of living with God near us then gives us security so we can be real with God, ourselves, and others. Those are the first two motifs that unlock our Life with God.

I am so happy to tell you that the third and final motif of Life with God is enjoying life. Jesus came to bring us abundant life, and that life is a life of joy. The Bible consistently talks about three big benefits of Life with God: love, joy, and peace.[21] True joy should be experienced by everyone who is a child of God. Martin Luther, a famous pastor from the 1500s, wrote about that kind of joy in the quote that begins this chapter. There is deep joy in being rescued and restored and united with God! There is great joy in knowing you are completely known and unconditionally loved. There is joy in nature and beauty. There is joy in sacrifice and honor and respect.

If we're always sad and depressed, then that tells us we're missing something beautiful God has for us. His desire and design are that there would be a song playing in the background of our life—a motif—a musical theme that is full of joy. I'm not talking about the kind of joy that comes from ignoring your problems, like the vacant smile after smoking a joint. It's the kind of joy that is aware of the many spiritual blessings around us and the reality of how God is with us.

Joni Eareckson Tada suffered a tragic accident as a teen. She dove into Chesapeake Bay when she was seventeen years old and broke her neck. She became a quadriplegic who was in constant pain, but she learned to have joy in spite of her suffering. She wrote a poignant article on the fiftieth anniversary of her accident[22] and said these words:

> I don't think you could find a happier follower of Jesus than me. The more my paralysis helps me get disentangled from sin, the more joy bubbles up from within. I can't tell you how many nights I have lain in bed, unable to move, stiff with pain, and have whispered near tears, "Oh, Jesus, I'm so happy. So very happy in you!" God shares his joy on his terms only, and those terms call for us to suffer, in some measure, like his Son. I'll gladly take it.

Why Do God and Joy Go Together Like Peanut Butter and Jelly?

This whole topic of joy is not an easy one for me personally. I tend to focus on the negative more than the positive, so enjoying life is something I need God's help to do. One of the things that has helped me is remembering that God is always a powerful good in my life, regardless of what is happening around me. I can always enjoy gifts like His love for me, my place in His family, His plan for using me in this world, and His work to transform me into a person of goodness and love. These bring me joy when I think of them, and no matter what valley I'm walking through in life, joy is only a thought away!

> *You will show me the way of life,*
> *granting me the joy of your presence*
> *and the pleasures of living with you forever.*
>
> Psalms 16:11

God's Pure Goodness

Sometimes I get tired of the bad or mixed motives of people around me, especially those who have some kind of authority over me (bosses, government officials). These people are searching for their own desires. So instead, find joy in God, the One who is pure love with no shadow of selfish interest. No matter what is going on in my world, I can set aside time to be with God. In these times of quiet, I am often basking in the radiance of God's goodness, His love for me, and His perfect care for the details of my life. He cares for me like no one else can, because He fully knows me and all the details of my life. Our Father's ability to be everywhere at all times makes Him the most engaged friend possible. His purity makes Him the most beautiful person to be with. It is refreshing to focus my heart on God each day, and His presence triggers joy in my heart.

Treasures from God

Assuming you have taken the plunge with God and become a follower of Jesus (See Key 1!), you can find unbounded joy in the gifts of forgiveness, eternal life, and the Holy Spirit in your heart. These are incredibly valuable gifts that were freely given to us from God—at great cost to Him. What value could we put on having all our mistakes and selfishness washed away? How much would you pay to spend eternity with God in a place filled with infinite love and joy and peace? What would you trade to have God's own Spirit connected to yours for all eternity? These treasures cannot even be measured! They are beyond our imagination, yet they are true!

If someone gives you a dollar, you may forget about it soon. When you're telling a friend about your day, you might not even remember to tell them about it. But if someone gives you a million dollars, you would never forget it. It is life-changing. It is unimaginably generous. It is unforgettable. You will definitely tell your friend about it! The gifts of God are so generous, so transformational, so unexpected that we should be filled with joy whenever we think of them. God's special gifts bring us joy. Receiving and remembering those gifts can turn up the soundtrack of joy in your life.

How Does Joy Energize Our Lives?

> *Don't be dejected and sad, for the joy of the LORD is
> your strength!*
>
> Nehemiah 8:10

You have probably experienced that when you don't have joy,
you can feel wiped out. When you do have joy, it is energizing. The
joy of the Lord is our strength! God's infusion of joy in our lives
lifts us up, even when life circumstances threaten to bring us down.

One of the happiest memories of
my childhood is doing flips on a
trampoline. I would play for hours,
then run home, crumple into our
sofa, and fall asleep. The pulsing
energy from joy kept me jumping

until I was completely spent. That's the way joy works. The joy of
the Lord is our strength, and we can always turn our hearts toward
God and reignite the joy that lifts us up.

How Does Joy Make God Look Good?

Joy is an important part of what it means to find Life with God.
In the 1600s there was a movement to revive faith and realign it
with the Bible. This movement was called the Reformation, and it
was a response to the sad reality that the Church had lost its way
in some places over the previous centuries. God called people to

rethink Life with God and turn back to the essentials that Jesus taught.

Leaders in the Reformation thought about what the ultimate purpose of Life with God is. Their answer has joy in it.

> Man's chief end is to glorify God and enjoy him forever.
>
> Westminster Short Confession

Let me translate it into modern language, because what it means is so powerful. What is the best thing a person can do with their life? **Praise God and enjoy Him forever.**

Joy is a part of Life with God. When it is a motif in our life, we are enjoying God and His gifts of love. We are enjoying whatever is good and pure and helpful. And so, there's true joy in our lives. There's a happiness that fills us. People will be drawn to us, because they sense the supernatural joy that's coming from us. And God intends for us to have joy!

This should be a background theme, a musical motif that fills up our lives with songs of joy. God brings joy into our lives in many ways, but the deepest ways are not dependent on anything in this world. Some of these channels for joy are:

- Knowing who we are as God's kids

- Accepting His forgiveness

- Learning that Our Father will never leave us

- Anticipating that we will be with Him when our physical body dies

- Experiencing God's Spirit connected with our own spirit

Δ Δ Δ Δ Δ Δ Δ Δ Δ Δ Δ Δ Δ Δ Δ Δ

And so Father, grant this dear reader
a little more joy today!

Δ Δ Δ Δ Δ Δ Δ Δ Δ Δ Δ Δ Δ Δ Δ Δ

SUM (KEY 3 MOTIFS)

Motifs are the background music of life, affecting how we do everything. We **ARE** abiding, being real, and enjoying!

Abiding is staying aware and connected to God throughout the day.

Being **R**eal means we are honest with God, ourselves, and others, even when it's risky.

Enjoying means appreciating God and the blessings of life.

Can you see how the bold letters in these three motifs spell A-R-E? The phrase "We are . . ." helps us remember the daily music of a God-centered life: We A-R-E Abiding, being Real, and Enjoying abundant life!

So far in this book we've talked about starting Life with God through a miracle by choosing Jesus, then focusing on the two missions of Jesus, and finally on the three motifs of Life with God. Next, we want to go deeper into what Jesus' perfect love looks like. His balanced, loving approach to life is our fourth Key: measures of love.

Questions to Help You Thrive

1. How much joy is in your daily life?

2. Do God and joy go together in your thinking, or do you need a shift in perspective to connect them?

3. How would you explain to a ten-year-old why it makes sense that God and joy in our lives are inevitably connected?

4. Was there an event when you felt the energy of joy give you the ability to do so much more because you were so happy?

5. Stop and pray, asking God to direct your thoughts. Which one of the avenues for joy is God putting on your heart after reading this chapter?

Resources for a Deeper Dive

- *Surprised by Joy,* by C.S. Lewis

- *Power in Praise,* by Merlin R. Carothers

Measures

The love of Jesus has a beautiful balance. Jesus perfectly balances time for healing, time for teaching, time with His disciples, time alone with His Father, and time for rest. Jesus lives in the hub of competing demands—just like you do.

Jesus' life shows activities that can be placed into four categories: growing, caring, serving, and sharing. The Measures Key is about checking these same measures in your own life. Our Measures Key graphic has ruler markings to remind us that they can be measured and observed. You can examine your life to see if you are finding balance in these four parts of a joyful God's love.

You might want to read about the Measures Key if:

- You want a practical evaluation of how your life reflects Jesus' calling

- You feel like your life is out of balance, too focused on one thing instead of finding God's best

- You don't understand why all these four measures should be part of Life with God

MEASURE: GROWING Δ

> O taste and see how good the Lord is! Blessed is the soul
> that clings wholly to Him! And the more it clings,
> the more it tastes of the sweetness of the Lord.
> (Bernard of Clairvaux, 12th century)

These four measures of Life with God are drawn from Jesus' life and show us what God's love is like. Each person will have favorites of these four aspects of love. Some of us are drawn to times alone with God, and we think, "Oh, this is so great! This is what Life with God is all about." Others of us may say, "Times in community, laughing and talking with my brothers and sisters—that's the part that really helps me." I find that my favorites change over time as God changes me.

So, each of us will need to overcome this natural imbalance if we want to embrace the fullness of Life with God. We will need to make an effort to do what may feel uncomfortable to mature in all four dimensions of love: growing, caring, serving, and sharing. Let's start with the first measure: growing.

What Does *Growing* Mean?

When we talk about growing, we mean a specific kind of spiritual growth: becoming closer and closer in relationship with God. We increase our understanding and experience of who God is, having gone through both good and hard times with God as our close friend. We trust Him more and follow His directions in more areas of our life. We rely on Him more for emotional support and guidance. We more frequently depend on His power when we are helping others. We come to feel His love and forgiveness deeply, just like we would if He were physically present with us.

One picture of mature growth that the Bible uses frequently is a tree becoming rooted in the soil of God's extravagant love. There's a beautiful verse in Ephesians, where the pastor is praying for his people, and he writes this:

> *Then Christ will make his home in your hearts as you trust in him, and your roots will grow down into God's love and keep you strong.*
>
> Ephesians 3:17

The image this verse creates shows our roots growing deep down into the soil of God's love, which has the nutrients we need to thrive! The cover of this book is inspired by this idea. God becomes a beloved mentor in our life—not just a force, not just the One who tells us what's right or wrong, not just the One we follow from afar, but a person we love and admire and want to imitate. Eventually, God becomes more of a close, connected friend than even our BFF or spouse.

Now I want you to think of the person you love the  most in this world.

When you begin to love God more than that person, then you've got the ideal depth of love for God.

Now I'm kind of crazy about Gayleen, my wife. She's kind and smart and thoughtful. Every year on our anniversary I thank God for another year with her. So, in my own spiritual life, I ask myself this question: "Do I love God more than I love Gayleen?" And that has challenged me through the years (We have dated since high school!). In my twenties I started asking myself that question, and the answer was clearly "No." I could lie to myself and say I loved God more, but the level of love and affection and enjoyment I felt for Gayleen outweighed what I felt for God by a lot.

I'm happy to say that, through the years, my love for God has grown. My love for Gayleen has also grown, but I finally realized that I was relying on Gayleen in some unhealthy ways in those early years. I want to cherish and please God more than Gayleen. God is always ready to interact, even when Gayleen is not present or is emotionally unavailable because of her own struggles. Gayleen is an amazing person, but God is even more amazing and loving and powerful, and He is worthy of my greatest, deepest affection and love.

Are You Growing Closer to God?

How about you? Is your love for God growing in a real way? Do you think about pleasing God more often than you once did? When you have problems in your life, is prayer your first response? Do you think "I've got to talk with God about this right away" when you feel rejected or hurt? Do you search in your Bible to find answers to your questions about what is best in your life?

This is how getting closer to God can revolutionize your life. He can be the One that helps you in every situation. He is always available when we need Him! Being connected to God also makes us able to love others better, because our needs are being met. Instead of being needy and angry with those around me, I can love them with God's love. So, the most important thing about loving others is being loved by God and growing closer and closer to Him.

Prayer

Two things are crucial to anyone who wants more of God. The first one is prayer, which starts with just talking to God. If you think prayer is something else besides conversation with God, you're making it too complicated. Don't worry about expressing yourself in fancy words like your pastor does. Say it how you would tell your best friend. There are no right or wrong words. God is our safest place—just pour your heart out to God.

You don't even have to talk to God out loud. You can pray by thinking what you would say to Him. God is everywhere and knows everything, and He hears your thoughts. So, you can just say words in your mind and connect with the heart of God! My friend, just pour out your heart. Take your troubles to Him. Take your worries to Him. Take your joys to Him. Then listen to His heart in quiet and sense His kindness, care, and guidance.

God also puts a big priority on the frequency of prayer. He says, "Never stop praying."[23] Never stop? Riiiiiight . . . I'll get right on that. There's a high bar set for us—a life goal! It's the essence of true abiding, so it does make sense.

The Bible

Besides talking to God in prayer, we have one other powerful way to grow closer to Him: His Word. In the Bible we hear God speaking to us. We learn to hear His voice, to distinguish it from our own voice and the voices of others that we carry inside us (like our parents' voices). In the Bible we learn about God's way, what pleases Him, and what He's like. We learn how people make mistakes and how to find God's forgiveness. We learn how to pray and how to complain to God and how to praise Him. We learn that He created everything and knows everything and is everywhere. God will speak to you through the Bible if you ask Him to help you hear. The Holy Spirit in you will help you hear God's voice in the words of the Bible, making them come alive. Isn't that amazing! We don't just talk to God. He talks to us!

The Bible is the very breath of God. God used people to write the Bible, but the co-Author along with each human writer was the Holy Spirit. The Holy Spirit ensured the writers were communicating God's heart in a book for all the people of the world. Listen to what God says about the Bible in these verses.

> *All Scripture is inspired by God and is useful to teach us what is true and to make us realize what is wrong in our lives. It corrects us when we are wrong and teaches us to do what is right. God uses it to prepare and equip his people to do every good work.*
>
> 2 Timothy 3:16–17

Why Do We Need BOTH Prayer and the Bible?

It's not enough to only pray. Your mind needs to be renewed by the Word of God. Your soul needs to be cleansed by His truth.

Sometimes people will tell me, "God told me blah-blah-blah." But I know God would never say that, because the message contradicts the Bible. God is not like a person who changes His views on topics. To get closer to God, we need both prayer and the truth of the Bible.

And the same is true for those who love the Bible but don't pray a lot. It's not enough to know the truth of the Bible without experiencing the power of interacting with God. There's a difference between knowing about someone and knowing them. Knowing that God is our helper in times of trouble is not meaningful if we don't actually talk with Him in times of trouble and let Him rescue us. The Bible is meant to guide us so we can know how to interact with God. It's not enough to know we are forgiven. We need to hear God forgive us through His words to us, and those words are in the Bible. That is an amazing gift! We can know who God is and what the most important things in life are by reading the Bible. The Bible is where we find the keys to Life with God.

Jesus shows us that we need both prayer and the Bible, because He prioritized both. The Bible says that Jesus often went off to a solitary place to pray. What?!? Jesus had to pray? He needed solo time? Yes! Jesus often slipped away from the crowds and His friends to pray alone. So, if He needs solo time to pray, I definitely need it. I need to be in solitary places to pray. Jesus also quoted long passages of Scripture when He spoke or was tempted. He quoted the Bible. He memorized the Bible. He showed us how important God's Word is in daily life. Jesus even compared the Bible to food—we need it to survive.

*People do not live by bread alone, but by every word
that comes from the mouth of God.*

Matthew 4:4

A growing relationship with God also means we grow in trusting Him more. When we read in the Bible that we should do something, we believe that is the very best thing to do, and we try to live that way as much as we can. Remember that we will often fail at being like Jesus, but we believe His way is the best and ask for His help to live that way. We decide that God's way is best even when we don't completely understand why. We eventually stop trying to figure out if God's way is best, and we simply trust Him. We are still broken and selfish at times, but we increasingly trust Him, and this opens our heart to transformation by the Holy Spirit. Our trust (a.k.a. faith) is the open door for God's power to continually change us.

Quiz Time!

Here is a tool you can use to help you see growth in your relationships with other believers. If filling it out makes you feel uncomfortable, don't use it. You have my permission to skip it! If you're interested, you can come back and fill it out again to measure your growth.

Answer each statement with a number from 0 to 4.

0 almost never || 1 infrequently || 2 half the time
3 most of the time || 4 almost always

1. I am aware of God's presence through my day.

2. I read the Bible to hear God's voice every day.

3. When I read something in the Bible, I try to live that way.

4. I talk with God in prayer about what I read in the Bible.

5. When there is a problem, I always pray first.

6. I enjoy taking solo time each day to simply be with God.

7. As I go through my day, I am thinking about doing what will bring joy to God's heart.

Questions to Help You Thrive

1. What does the word *growing* remind us to do?

2. Who is one of your closest friends? How does that relationship compare to your relationship with God?

3. What about prayer is easy for you? Hard for you?

4. What helps you hear God's voice as you read the Bible?

5. Why do you need both prayer and the Bible to grow in your love for God?

Resources for a Deeper Dive

- *The Return of the Prodigal Son*, by Henri Nouwen

- *The Sacred Romance*, by Brent Curtis and John Eldredge

MEASURE: CARING Δ

Work together with each other; pull in unison;
run together; suffer together; sleep together; and awake
together, as the heirs, and associates, and servants of God.
(Ignatius of Antioch, 2nd century)

The first measure of God's love in our lives is **growing** closer with God. The second measure is **caring** for others in the family of God.

What Does *Caring* Mean?

When we talk about caring, we mean living in community with those who are on a faith journey in our local church. Ignatius of Antioch was a church leader who wrote a description of what it meant to be part of the community of God almost 2,000 years ago. This ancient quote still rings true today. Caring for others in our church community means working together, relying on each other's strengths, sharing our sufferings, spending time together beyond casual friendships, listening to God's directions, and helping each other serve Him.

> *All the believers met together in one place and shared everything they had.*
>
> Acts 2:44

When I think of true community, I'm reminded of a couple in our church family whose house burned down. They were devastated, especially since they lost a dear pet in the accident. Our church community gathered around them and cried with them, prayed for them, raised money for the extra expenses they had, and put together work parties to help with temporary housing on their property. I was so proud of our people, seeing them love as the hands and feet of God in a moment of crisis—and it meant the world to the couple! This is a true expression of community.

God designed each of us with a need for community. We need to be genuinely known by others—finding out that people love and accept us even when they know us. We need people who care for us and check in on us. When we are lost and discouraged, they are there to help us. When our hearts are so twisted and upset that we can't hear the God talking to us, they speak the words of God wrapped in a hug. We need others who help us grow in areas that are blind spots, while still loving us through our struggles. That is also true community.

Did Jesus Need Community?

Do you notice that in the biographies of Jesus (Matthew, Mark, Luke, and John), there is always community around Jesus? He was part of the Jewish community. He participated in His local synagogue all the time, taking turns reading the Bible and speaking with Jewish teachers about the Bible.

When Jesus was thirty years old and began his public ministry, His first priority was to pick twelve disciples to mentor closely. These people became His small group and travelled everywhere with Him. Jesus had a larger group of disciples too. His friends Mary and Martha and lots of other people were His disciples.

If Jesus needed community, then you and I need community even more. He had a perfect relationship with God. He knew who He was and why He was on earth. He was completely at peace as an individual, and yet He still enjoyed community—and so should we! (Except if someone is a Dodgers' fan)

What Are the Barriers to Community for Americans?

Relying on others is something that's difficult for us as Americans, because we tend to be self-sufficient people. We value independence so much that we often struggle with community. The truth is that most of us need more community. People are often lonely, especially among our young people and our senior adults. We need healthy, nurturing relationships. So, if we are made for God's type of caring community, and if it brings us so many benefits, what are the barriers? What's holding us back?

Barrier 1: Time

Most of us are very busy. This is especially true for families with young kids in school. Homework, sports, dance class, music practice, visits to relatives, vacations—it's a lot! These parts of our lives are often shouting "I need more!" We have relatives who want to see us. We have dreams of getting a degree or starting a new business. Our jobs want more time from us. Our kids need more time with us. We need more time with God. AND we need to relax—Ready . . . RELAX NOW! Ugh. Juggling all of these time demands is hard.

It's easy to allow these pressures to set our priorities, but we need to let God do that. He knows what's best for us and for those we love. And God believes in being in community.

Let us think of ways to motivate one another to acts of love and good works. And let us not neglect our meeting together, as some people do, but encourage one another, especially now that the day of his return is drawing near.

                                                    Hebrews 10:24-25

God calls us to "not neglect our meeting together" and to make a commitment to our local church community. I have seen families that prioritize sports over church, and soon they are only marginally involved in the church community. Later they are surprised when their young adult children don't see the value in attending church. This is the same priority the parents modeled for them, so the kids learned it from their parents who are now regretting their choices. The enemy of our souls, the evil one (commonly called the devil or satan), knows that keeping people out of a faith community is a very effective way of stunting their spiritual life.

So, we must put God first in our life and make spiritual community a priority—even if our feelings say we don't have time.

Barrier 2: Selfishness

This barrier is as old as humanity! Part of our brokenness is to think of ourselves first. That's called selfishness. We often think of our own needs before the needs of others. Community is hard, because we have to value the group as much as we value ourself.

The truth is that community gives more than it takes. We soon learn we gain so much in community that what we give up is small in comparison. Pastor Paul talked about this dynamic in a letter to a church community 2,000 years ago:

> *Is there any encouragement from belonging to Christ? Any comfort from his love? Any fellowship together in the Spirit? Are your hearts tender and compassionate? Then make me truly happy by agreeing wholeheartedly with each other, loving one another, and working together with one mind and purpose. Don't be selfish; don't try to impress others. Be humble, thinking of others as better than yourselves. Don't look out only for your own interests, but take an interest in others, too.*
>
> Philippians 2:1–4

Don't be selfish, but be humble instead. Don't try to impress other people, but instead serve them and highlight their contributions. Don't try to always get your own way, but realize when God is calling the church to go in another direction. Support the leaders of the church and honor them. Open your heart to what your Core Group pastor (small group pastor, more on this ahead!) says to you about growing spiritually. Care for people in your church community who can't give back to you, those EGR (Extra Grace Required) people who often annoy others. Rely on the supernatural love of God flowing through you, and obey His call to sacrifice self for community.

Barrier 3: Digital Isolation

As the digital world expands in our culture, we spend more time online and less connecting with others in real life (IRL). In a digital space it's possible to portray ourselves in any way we wish, so we can be someone we're not. We all know the danger a sexual predator presents by pretending to be a child, but this kind of deception is only possible because the digital world allows us to pretend to be someone we're not.

When online, we need to be honest about how we present ourselves. This means being self-aware, knowing our strengths and weaknesses, and ignoring the invisibility cloak in online interactions that often leads us to deceive others. It requires maturity and honest feedback and a solid identity as God's child, since it's easier to present carefully groomed appearances in digital interactions.

We need the accountability of IRL relationships and godly community that accepts us as we are instead of as we wish we were.

Why Do We Need Community?

When we overcome these barriers, we discover the richness of community. There is sacrifice and iron-sharpening-iron and EGR (Extra Grace Required) people, but as we grow together there is so much good! We find a safe place where we are loved for who we are. We find a

Better Together!

place where we can learn to love in a community that embraces everyday forgiveness. We find guidance and encouragement and honest feedback to unlock a deeper Life with God.

As more of an introvert than an extrovert, I feel the cost of community in the amount of energy it costs to be with others. I enjoy people and love to talk and laugh with them as their pastor and friend, but I'm tired when my day is over.

So, as someone who is aware of the cost of community, I want to encourage you with this: God blesses me through community more often than when I'm alone. I share a burden with someone, and the heaviness is lightened as she prays for me. In the middle of an animated discussion, God breaks through, and I sense His guidance for my own life. When working together, a group can work in a way that maximizes the strengths of the group and minimizes the weaknesses. Supernatural moments of growth often happen in community, since we are close to the heart of God when we are among His children.

I love the joke that if you ever find a perfect church community, don't join it. You'll ruin it! Yep! So, resign yourself to joining a group of people like you: broken but growing. Throw yourself into a bunch of people exploring Life with God. You will make mistakes and have conflict and learn to lean on Jesus and learn the beauty of being part of a group of God's kids. You will also find acceptance and mentors and God among His kids in a special way.

How Should We Support Our Local Church?

The first step is to commit to a local church and spend time building relationships there each week. I still vividly remember a conversation with a man from our church community who asked me, "Why are all my *real* friends outside the church? In fact, the people I trust most are the ones I grew up with, not the people in this church!" There was frustration in his realization, because we talk a lot about community at our church. I asked him how much time he had spent with his childhood friends. "Thousands of hours, I'm sure. We just hung out all day when we were kids."

"And how many hours have you spent with people in our church community?" I asked.

"Well, I'm really busy now, and . . ." You know, community takes time and effort, and bonding happens unexpectedly in the midst of sharing life together. You have to invest time to build true community.

Another step is to support your church by volunteering there regularly. Help out with welcoming and seating people. Help teach the kids. Help keep the property maintained. Work on the Tech Team that runs the sound system and does video production.

Write cards to celebrate the birthdays of people in your church community. Visit those who are in the hospital or homebound. Help others in your church community.

Finally, support your church by giving to God from your finances. The Bible calls every follower of Jesus to give back to God regularly. A good goal from the Bible is to give ten percent of your income to help your church and the needy. Regular percentage-based giving means that you give more as God blesses you financially, and it keeps the love of money from taking over your life. Support your local church community by giving your treasure to God through your church.

Quiz Time!

Here is a tool you can use to help you see growth in your relationships with other believers. If filling it out makes you feel uncomfortable, don't use it. You have my permission to skip it! If you're interested, you can come back and fill it out again to measure your growth.

Answer each statement with a number from 0 to 4.

0 almost never || 1 infrequently || 2 half the time
3 most of the time || 4 almost always

1. I attend a worship service almost every week.

2. I attend a weekly small group, which discusses Life with God.

3. I meet with people from my church community outside

of church activities at least once a month.

4. I am committed to sharing my true struggles with people in my church community, even when it makes me feel vulnerable.

5. I am in a helping role to encourage at least two others in our church community to grow in their Life with God.

6. I help support our church by giving a percentage of my income to them.

7. I pray every week for the needs of people in our church community.

Questions to Help You Thrive

1. What does the word *caring* remind us to do?

2. What challenges do you foresee when you think of teaming with other followers of Jesus?

3. Why is community part of following Jesus?

4. Which of the barriers to community affects you the most?

5. How is God calling you to open yourself to a more caring community today?

Resources for a Deeper Dive

- *Called to Community (2nd Edition),* edited by Charles E. Moore

- "Four Types of Community We All Need," video by Practicing the Way

MEASURE: SERVING △

> One of the principal rules of religion is, to miss no occasion
> of serving God. And, since He is invisible to our eyes, we are
> to serve Him in our neighbor; which He receives as if done to
> Himself in person, standing visibly before us.
> (John Wesley, 18th century)

The first of our measures of God's love is **growing** in our relationship with God. This is the source of our love and power and identity. The next measure is **caring** for other believers in community. True community helps us experience the same Spirit working through many hearts, and this encourages and enables us to be part of God's family on earth. The third measure of God's love in our lives is **serving**.

What Does *Serving* mean?

Serving is something very specific. You might say, "Well, I'm serving as an usher in my local church," but that's not the kind of serving we're talking about with this measure. Do you see that we're taking each of these general words (growing, caring, and serving) and making them very specific (growing in relationship with God and caring for other believers in your local church)? Serving means **serving people outside your church community**.

We want to help a neighbor mow his weeds. We want to take a friend out to dinner for her birthday. We want to provide a safe place to sleep for a person who is unhoused. We go shopping for a person who is homebound. We listen to people who are suffering with mental health  issues. We strive to be the kind of people that others count on when they need help. That is why meeting needs outside of our church community is so important to living out our faith. That's why serving is one of our four measures in Life with God.

Why is Serving a Mark of God's Presence in Us?

The short answer is this: serving is the antidote to selfishness.

Selfishness is the curse of every human heart. We naturally tend to do the things that benefit ourselves—the activities that make our bank accounts grow, that increase our reputation among those we want to impress. This tendency is why seeing genuine serving surprises (even shocks) others and marks followers of Jesus as different.

We can feel in awe of those who live giving lives, but when we are growing and caring it is so much easier—God and our church community are meeting deep needs. We should be able to understand Mother Teresa and her devotion to the sick in India, or Ignatius of Loyola who left a wealthy family to become a poor priest and help young men be established in their faith, or Jesus (God in human form) coming to serve us by suffering and dying on a cross. Selfless devotion is often a mark of God's abundant life in a soul. It is a fruit of a thriving Life with God.

As I've already mentioned, I am more introverted than extroverted, and I experience God's presence and words easily when I am alone. I am naturally drawn to long times of silence and fasting and prayer on retreat. I also enjoy the community of those who are exploring Life with God. There is a bond so deep between followers of Jesus! Even when I have gone overseas to places where I don't speak the language, I have experienced profound connection with God's people through hand motions, smiles, and a few shared words spoken. In my life, growing and caring happen easily.

Serving, on the other hand, is not easy for me. I watch my church friends with amazement as they serve selflessly with ease. For me, it is hard to serve when there is little thanks for what I'm doing. Meeting the needs of others has become a priority more recently in my spiritual journey. At my core, I am trying to let God transform my selfishness into service, but it is a slow process. It's good for me to regularly serve in unremarkable ways that do not get affirmed.

Serving allows God's work in my heart—removing another layer of selfishness and helping me learn to enjoy unrecognized service. I serve at a food pantry and most of the people coming in speak only Spanish. Since I'm not bilingual, I'm really only good for putting carrots and potatoes in a bag or carrying a crate of lettuce from the refrigerator. Others are in charge and I'm just a flunky. That's great for me, and I have learned to just say "Jesus, this is for you" when I serve.

Did Jesus Serve Others?

When we read about the life of Jesus in the Bible, one of the shocking things we learn about Him is how humble He is. Two stories I want to share show Jesus' commitment to humble service. Both happen at the very end of His life on earth, when He was preparing His followers for when He would no longer be with them in person.

In the final week before Jesus dies, two of his disciples are trying to earn a special honor over the rest of the disciples. This creates jealousy and anger among the group, but Jesus deflates all this prideful jousting by refocusing them.

> *So Jesus called them together and said, "You know that the rulers in this world lord it over their people, and officials flaunt their authority over those under them. But among you it will be different. Whoever wants to be a leader among you must be your servant, and whoever wants to be first among you must be the slave of everyone else. For even the Son of Man came not to be*

served but to serve others and to give his life as a ransom for many."

Mark 10:42–45

The people Jesus honors are people who serve others, just as Jesus did. Even though He was God, Jesus uses the title "Son of Man" to refer to Himself, and even Jesus did not come to BE served, but to serve others. As His followers, we choose to serve others like He did!

The second story about Jesus' surprising commitment to serving happens on Jesus' last night before His crucifixion. Before His last meal with the disciples, Jesus does one of the dirtiest jobs in the ancient world. There were no toilets to clean back  in Jesus' day, but people did walk around in sandals through dirt and animal dung and if they were fishermen, fish guts. When people came together for a fancy meal, a servant would wash everyone's nasty feet before the meal. And in this key moment Jesus made an impression on His disciples they would never forget.

Jesus knew that the Father had given him authority over everything and that he had come from God and would return to God. So he got up from the table, took off his robe, wrapped a towel around his waist, and poured water into a basin. Then he began to wash the disciples' feet, drying them with the towel he had

around him. . . . After washing their feet, he put
on his robe again and sat down and asked, "Do you
understand what I was doing? You call me 'Teacher'
and 'Lord,' and you are right, because that's what I
am. And since I, your Lord and Teacher, have washed
your feet, you ought to wash each other's feet. I have
given you an example to follow. Do as I have done to
you."

John 13:3–5, 12–15

Jesus was the humble servant who did the dirtiest jobs to meet the needs of others, and so we inherit this calling from Him as His followers. He's asking us to be like Him in serving others. I love how Jesus knew He had all authority over everything and was returning to be with God, and how this knowledge of His place of honor and destiny triggered His serving. Do you see the paradox of this? Being secure in His identity and future, Jesus served. So can we! We also know our identity and future, and so we can serve like Jesus. Let me rewrite these words for myself. I encourage you to try this with your own name too.

Theo knew that the Father had adopted him into His family. One day when he died, Theo would return to be with God forever. So, Theo followed the example of Jesus on this earth and served others, finding needs and meeting them in love. He listened to people who talked too much and helped hand out food at a nonprofit in his town and fixed his neighbor's mailbox when it fell down. (Adapted from John 13)

There's something very, very special about looking outside of ourselves, finding somebody who has a clear need, and then meeting that need. It's weed whacking your neighbor's yard. It's sending a person who's lost their pet a sympathy card or note. It's standing up for a coworker who is being sexually harassed. It's listening to someone you just met who is having a tough day and needs to process. Service is a visible sign of God's love in us.

Why Does God Care So Much About the Poor and Needy?

One of the themes of the Bible is how God cares for the poor and needy. God cares for the widow with no children. God cares for the family struggling to put food on the table. God cares for the child working twelve hours a day for no pay in the coffee fields. God cares for the prisoner who never has a visitor. God's love moves us to bring help to these who need it most.

When Jesus talked about the Day of Judgement, the day He evaluates our lives at the end of time, the poor and needy are center stage.[24] To some of us He will say, "Thank you for the times that you came and fed me. Thank you for the times that you came and visited me when I was in prison. Thank you for the times you came and cared for me." Then we will say to Jesus, "Jesus, I've never fed You? When did we come and care for You?" And Jesus is going to say, "When you did it to the least of those around you, you did it to Me. When you cared for those people that our world does not care about, then you cared for Me."

I want to hear Jesus say that to me when He evaluates my life. Do you? Do you want to be someone who serves like Jesus did? And are you known as a person who helps? Be a person who shines with divine light through your unselfish service to others. When you help them, you are helping Jesus!

Quiz Time!

Here is a tool to help you see growth in serving people outside your church community. If filling it out makes you feel uncomfortable, don't use it. You have my permission to skip it! If you're interested, you can come back and fill it out again to check your growth in this area.

Answer each statement with a number from 0 to 4.

0 almost never || 1 infrequently || 2 half the time
3 most of the time || 4 almost always

1. At least once a month I am meeting a need of someone outside my church community.

2. When I see a neighbor, I know their name and the basics about their family.

3. I am aware of the most common struggles people have in our town or city.

4. I ask other people in our church community how they serve others.

5. When I see someone in obvious need (unhoused, high or drunk, asking for help), my gut reaction is compassion.

6. I am willing to serve, even when there is no gratitude or recognition for my work.

7. I pray for God to show me what needs to meet and which ones to let go.

Questions to Help You Thrive

1. What does the word *serving* remind us to do?

2. Why does Jesus say we serve Him when we serve others?

3. Jesus washed feet—what is the modern equivalent of that dirty job?

4. How does serving help fight selfishness?

5. Where do you feel God's compassion pushing you to meet needs?

Resources for a Deeper Dive

- *In His Steps,* by Charles Sheldon

- *Celebration of Discipline*, by Richard Foster ("Service" chapter)

MEASURE: SHARING △

> Preach the Gospel always, and if necessary, use words.
> (Francis of Assisi, 12th century)

S o, now we've got our first three measures in Life with God: **growing**, **caring**, and **serving**. The last of our four measures is **sharing**—sharing Life with God with other people. In the quote above by Francis of Assisi, the "Gospel" means the powerful reality of how Jesus opened the way to God for us. He urges us to model Life with God in what we do, and when needed, to use words to describe it to others. That's what I want to tell you about in this chapter: **sharing** our great treasure, Jesus, with others who need Him. This chapter is about how love guides our actions and words to help those who need Life with God.

Live wisely among those who are not believers,
and make the most of every opportunity. Let your
conversation be gracious and attractive so that you will
have the right response for everyone.

Colossians 4:5–6

Wow. Oh, OK . . . I just need to have the right response for *everyone*. No pressure here. Yikes! So, how do we live wisely and have a right response for those who need Jesus?

Why Should I Share My Faith?

The first idea I want to repeat is this: only share your faith with people you love. Forget offering spiritual guidance to those in your life that you don't love. I know God wants us to love everybody, but if that's not where you're at with someone, you might want to keep your faith to yourself for now. Let your Life with God change your heart until you share God's love for that person.

On the other hand, for those you love, no treasure is more valuable than Life with God. Nothing can make more of a positive change in their life on this earth, and nothing can make such a dramatic difference in eternity. Life with God is literally the best gift anyone can receive in this world. So, when we love someone, we want them to have it. Jesus gave us this image:

Again, the Kingdom of Heaven is like a merchant on
the lookout for choice pearls. When he discovered a

*pearl of great value, he sold everything he owned and
bought it!*

Matthew 13:45–46

When Jesus uses the term
"Kingdom of Heaven," He means
Life with God—the pearl of greatest
value! There are other good things in
life, like love, family, character, and
loyalty. But none of them have the
fullness and depth and value and joy
of Life with God. The joy we find

in Life with God mixes with the love we have for our friends to
motivate us to share the Way, the Truth, and the Life (Jesus!).

What's the Best Way to Share My Faith?

The best way to share your faith is really simple—just talk about
what God is doing in your life. Sharing our faith is a combination
of all of the motifs in Key 3: abide (stay connected), be real (share
honestly about what God is doing), and enjoy (share the joy that
God is bringing into your life).

The followers of Jesus in the Bible did this over and over again.
They shared what God was doing in their life with others. They
used stories and pictures to share about the miracle of having the
Holy Spirit in their hearts. It can be the same for you. If you are
growing and caring and serving God, then the Holy Spirit is doing
great things in your life. Just share about what that is. Just be real
with people about how God is meeting your needs and helping you

be less selfish. You don't need to make things up. If you cannot honestly share about the difference God makes in your life, you may need to prioritize getting your relationship right with God! Make sure you have the Holy Spirit (Key 1) and are experiencing the love of God in your life (Keys 2 and 3).

How Can I Tell Them About the Miracle That Starts It All?

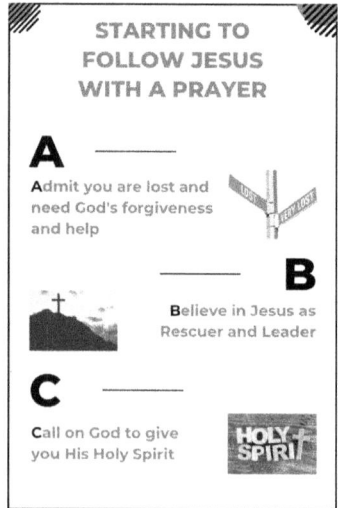

You should also be ready to share how the person you love can pray for God to enter their lives and put His Spirit into them. Giving them this book might be a good step, if they are a reader or listener (audiobook). All the basics of turning your life over to God and becoming a follower of Jesus are contained in the ABCs.

This can help you remember the basics when someone wants God in their life. A big hope I have in writing this book is to make it easy to explain how to follow Jesus to another person, by telling them about the 5 Keys to Life with God. I want you to be able to describe Life with God in a way that's simple and clear and compelling.

What if I Don't Want to Share My Faith?

Let me talk about the difficulties of sharing our spiritual life with those who need Jesus. Few people naturally integrate their new spiritual health into their conversations with those who don't follow Jesus. I admire people who naturally share their faith from the start. For most of us, especially when we are around people hostile to God, we may feel it is too risky and awkward to share about spiritual things.

Here are some hurdles that you might feel about sharing what God is doing in you:

- Your friend may make fun of you, telling others you have become "all Jesus-y."

- You may not know the answers to questions that your friend has, like "Why did God allow my grandma to get cancer when she was such a good person?"

- You might not feel like your life is a good enough example of Life with God.

- You may feel exposed by sharing spiritual stories that are so intimate and meaningful to you.

- Sharing on a spiritual level is considered impolite conversation in many circles, so you are breaking social norms by talking about God.

Let me share two thoughts regarding these legitimate barriers. First, I have found that my fears about sharing my faith are overexaggerated. When I actually share my faith journey with someone I love, the person is usually interested. They may not agree with my viewpoint, but they are open to having me talk about what is happening in my life. They may even feel honored by such honest sharing.

The second insight is that real love overcomes these barriers. In the Resources section of this chapter, you can find help with any of these difficulties, but love and compassion for someone moves me to share openly about Jesus, to pray for them, to tell another beggar where to find food for the soul.

What Happens When People Share This Way?

This honest sharing is the way Jesus changed the world. Christianity started with a small group of people in one tiny, little city, and within 300 years it had spread to millions of people. Today it's the biggest religion in the entire world, because people were real about what God was doing in their lives. That's what sharing your faith means: tell others what God's doing. It's incredibly powerful.

It's also exciting. I find that when I'm praying for people who need Jesus, God speaks to me about ways to serve them or conversation topics to pursue. Then the next time I see them I am putting into practice what God has told me in prayer times. This reminds me that I'm partnering with God's work in calling this person to trust Jesus. It's fun to see God working in the lives of those we love!

So, invest time in loving people, praying for them, discovering their needs and helping them. Deep in their heart, they might wonder, "Is God there? Does He care for me?" I hope you could say to them, "God is a little bit like me, but much better!" And they would think, "Oh, that would be great if I had more people like you in my life." I know that if I bring that friend to my Core Group, they will meet people who have that same love of God in them. If I invite them to our worship service, they will hear about Life with God and be challenged to become a follower of Jesus. I know that they will see a life moving toward more serving and less selfishness.

Our Father is also passionate about seeing our friends find Life with Him. He wants them to know life *now* and life *in eternity* with Him. So, as we are sharing how God makes a difference in our life, we feel the pleasure of our Father who wants them to come home to Him. God changes the world one life at a time, and your sharing can make an eternal difference!

SUM (KEY 4 MEASURES)

Measures are the dimensions of God's love.

Growing in our love for God
Caring for others in our church community
Serving those outside our church community
Sharing our faith so others can find Life with God

Quiz Time!

Here is a tool to help you see growth in sharing your faith. If filling it out makes you feel uncomfortable, don't use it. You have my permission to skip it! If you're interested, you can come back and fill it out again to check your growth.

Answer each statement with a number from 0 to 4.

0 almost never || 1 infrequently || 2 half the time

3 most of the time || 4 almost always

1. I spend time at least once a month with a local person who doesn't follow Jesus yet.

2. I share spiritual stories from my life with those who need Jesus.

3. At least once a week I pray for two people who need Jesus.

4. I learn about answering faith questions (books, YouTube) regularly.

5. I could help a person who is ready know how to start a relationship with God.

6. I feel the longing that God has for those who do not know Him.

7. I feel like sharing my faith, because God makes such a difference in my own life.

Questions to Help You Thrive

1. What does the word *sharing* remind us to do?

2. Why should we only share our faith with those we love?

3. Do you connect sharing your faith with telling others what God is doing in your own life?

4. Could you explain how someone can pray to become a follower of Jesus (the ABCs!)? Practice your explanation.

5. What are the barriers to sharing your faith? Pray for God's Spirit to help you overcome these obstacles.

Resources for a Deeper Dive

- *Out of the Saltshaker and Into the World*, by Rebecca Manley Pippert

If you want more about answering objections to the Christian faith

- *Mere Christianity*, by C.S. Lewis

- *Confronting Christianity*, by Rebecca McLaughlin

Methods

N ow it's time to get really practical. You have learned about four Keys with ten different parts so far. Good job! Now, how do you live out this thriving Life with God when you work a job, are a parent, and want to have a social life, too?

I want to make sure you know that Life with God is not overwhelming. Our Methods Key graphic has a map on it, because these methods show you the actual route to Life with God. These methods will integrate the missions, motifs, and measures of love into your regular life.

We will talk about each method, how it connects to the other Keys, how often you should practice it, and then some tips.

You might want to read about the Methods Key if:

- You feel overwhelmed with trying to integrate everything you've learned in this book

- You are a detail person who needs to know practical steps to understand the big picture

- You resonate with everything we've talked about, but your own spiritual life is not flourishing

METHOD: DAILY CONNECTIONS Δ

To pray is to change.
Prayer is the central avenue God uses to transform us.
(Richard Foster, 21st century)

M y wife, Gayleen, is an impressive person! One of the challenges in her life, though, is being organized. She loves the idea of being organized. She loves the simplicity and ease when she's organized. She even loves binders and paper clips! But she is, by nature, organizationally challenged.

Like many others, she is overwhelmed with this life of too much stuff. Sometimes she will have 3,000+ personal emails unread. Sometimes mail starts to pile up or supplies for a project sit in a paper bag pushed under the table. She sets aside things to give to others, and they soon become a mountain. This bothers her more than it bothers anyone else in our family, but to change it she needed more than just motivational phrases ("A place for everything and everything in its place"). She needed a method—a practical plan. Gayleen learned a practical method from a person who has taught many others about overcoming clutter, and that is gradually transforming her inbox and desk. She is experiencing more joy and less stress because of this change.

The five methods described in this section are not new or unique to me. If they were, I would be suspicious of how successful they are at helping people find Life with God. After all, people have been following Jesus for thousands of years, and the same Holy Spirit has guided all of us. The only difference might be the resources we have today that they didn't have in AD 500, like the fact that we can own and read the Bible when those who followed Jesus in AD 500 could not afford one . . . and most people couldn't read! People in AD 500 had to go to a church service to hear the Bible, so they did that every day. Today we can listen to the words of God by reading the Bible ourselves.

As I introduce these five methods, there is an intentional order to them. I am starting with the method of most importance for a thriving Life with God. Then the second method is the second most important one, and so on. I am praying that you, like followers of Jesus for hundreds of years, will learn the power of these five spiritual habits and will let God into your life through them.

What Are the Daily Connections?

The Daily Connections are three spiritual habits to practice at different times throughout your day. Over the centuries, one of the practical things God's followers have needed for a Life with God is multiple reminders every day of God's presence, His love, and His resources. So, it's not surprising that our first method is about connecting with God three times each day: once in the morning as you first wake up (Good Morning God), then once during the day for ten to thirty minutes of Bible reading and prayer (Spiritual Boost), and then at night before going to sleep (Good Night Review). Doing these each day will change your life, because they keep you in God's presence, and being with Him changes us! Let's explain each one in the order you would do them in your day.

Good Morning God

Before you even put your feet on the floor in the morning, take two minutes to open your heart to God. Get a 3 x 5-inch card to put next to your bed. On the card you write out a simple prayer to God and a verse that will help you during your day. I have a bunch of these cards in the drawer beside my bed after using them for many years. Here is one of my Good Morning God cards from my drawer.

Verse: God says "If you look for Me wholeheartedly, you will find me." (Jer 29:13)

Prayer: God, I want to be aware of You in new ways in 2025. Please help me see You clearly today.

Enjoy: I pause now to enjoy _____

When you open your eyes, just grab that card. Sit a moment and become aware of God's presence with you. Say to God, "Father, speak to me through

Your Word." Read the verse and think about what it means. Maybe read it again. Then say the prayer from your heart and sit with God for a few seconds. Finally, finish your Good Morning God with joy by thinking of a blessing God has given you. Think about it until you feel the joy. Now you're ready to start your day! You will notice a huge difference in your days as you make this a regular part of each morning.

When your Good Morning God card loses "punch" for you, pick another verse that speaks to you. You might find this in the Bible message at church or a verse from a recent Spiritual Boost, or you can just google "popular Bible verses" and see how God is reaching others. Then write a short prayer to God for you to start the day. Fill out a new 3 x 5 card, and you are ready for tomorrow's Good Morning God.

If you want to learn more about the Good Morning God, it is referred to by different names through history. You can look for the words Morning Prayer, Lauds, or the Daily Office (which has both the Good Morning God and the Good Night Review).

Spiritual Boost

Sometime during your day, you set aside at least ten minutes for a Spiritual Boost. It could be sitting in your car before you go into work, or during your lunch break, or during your child's nap. This brings you into God's presence and feeds your mind and spirit on His words in the Bible. The two core parts of a Spiritual Boost time are prayer and Bible reading, but we will also talk about other activities you can add.

Prayer

Prayer is talking and listening to God. Every relationship needs shared communication, and as we deepen our Life with God, we get to know Him better and better. What makes prayer different than talking with our friends is that God is not contained in a body sitting across from us. He is everywhere around us and, when we become a follower of Jesus, lives in us through His Spirit. This means that we can speak or think and God hears us. It's amazing when you think of how close God is!

I like to start off my Spiritual Boost time with a question: What is on my heart today? This is the "being real" motif (Key 3) applied to prayer. I sit quietly and notice what is capturing my thoughts and emotions. Sometimes there is just peace, but usually there is something on my mind. I start my Spiritual Boost time by bringing this to our Father, talking about how I feel and what my concerns are. Sometimes I need to ask for forgiveness. Sometimes I need to talk through a problem and ask God for wisdom. Sometimes I need to leave a burden with God.

Then I move on to praying for people. Here I pray for the needs and work of God in the lives of those I love. I include loved ones in my immediate family and in my church community, those who care for others around the world, and those on my Sharing Life List (more about this later!). I have a rotation where each day I pick a different group to pray about: (Monday = my own spiritual growth, Tuesday = my church community, Wednesday = my family, Thursday = outreach ministries, Friday = Sharing

Life List, Saturday = government officials, Sunday = those I am mentoring)

After this, I often move into Bible reading with a prayer. *Holy Spirit, make these words alive in my heart as I read.* I'll talk more about Bible reading in the next section.

Finally, at the end of my Spiritual Boost, I often take time just to listen to God. At least one minute of silence, to just sit and allow God to bring things to mind for me. Sometimes he brings to mind the name of someone who needs help. Other times he gives me encouragement in an area of struggle. I pause to wait and listen.

Bible Reading

A very important step in hearing God's voice through Bible reading or listening is to use a modern and accurate translation of the Bible. Some of us have a Bible from someone who means a lot to us, and we want to use it out of respect for this person. However, using a modern translation helps us understand what God is saying more easily and accurately. Our church uses the New Living Translation (NLT), and this is a wonderful Bible to read during your Spiritual Boost time. Another good translation that is a bit harder to understand is the New International Version (NIV).

So, where should you read in your Bible? Many churches, including ours, have suggested places to read each day. On the back of the message notes, we have five Bible reading passages and one question to think about each day. If your church doesn't have this, a great place to start is with one of the biographies of Jesus—Matthew, Mark, Luke, or John. I recommend Luke for someone without much church background.

Just read until something grabs your heart and mind. Then stop and talk with God about what you are thinking. God will work in your mind and help you understand how you should interact with His words. One good tool for thinking about how to apply what you have read is the SWORD method (You can read how to use the SWORD method in the "Extra Stuff" section at the back of this book).

Add-Ons

Around this core of prayer and Bible reading (or listening to the Bible if you prefer), many other ways of connecting with God can be added. Here are a few that have helped people meet with God and get a Spiritual Boost in their day.

- Sing a worship song that you enjoy.

- Read a devotional book, where a person shares a Bible verse and what it means to them.

- Start a Spiritual Boost journal where you write the date, what you prayed about, and what you learned from the Bible verses you read. In our church we offer a journal with the SWORD method and other helps on the covers.

- Listen to a podcast of a sermon or talk that encourages your faith.

- Use an app like Lectio365 or the YouVersion Bible to help you during your Daily Connections.

The Spiritual Boost has been called different names through history, like Quiet Time, Morning Watch, or Daily Devotion.

Good Night Review

At the end of the day, as you're getting into bed, it's so great to finish the day in prayer. If you share that bed with a partner, you may need to let them know what you're doing! In just three to five minutes, you can do a Good Night Review.

The first question to think about is how you brought joy to God that day. When in my day did I choose God and please His heart with my love for Him and others?

I sit and mentally run through the day's events. I remember how often I was abiding in God, staying connected to Him. I remember when I didn't get angry with someone who required my patience. I remember times of victory over temptation. And I let the joy of God flow into my heart. There usually was good in this day because I let God work though me! Sit with the good feeling for a minute or two.

Then ask a second question. When in my day did I forget God and make mistakes?

Often my review of good moments of the day reminded me also of my failures. Now I consider those with God. For these times, I ask God for forgiveness, and I accept it. You can claim this verse if you are weighed down with guilt.

If we claim we have no sin, we are only fooling ourselves
and not living in the truth. But if we confess our sins to

*him, he is faithful and just to forgive us our sins and
to cleanse us from all wickedness.*

1 John 1:8–9

As followers of Jesus, we need to accept our failures, knowing that they don't define who we are. We are children of the King, and one day we'll live a glorious life with Him and always love everyone. In the meantime, Jesus died to provide forgiveness for our mistakes, and we rely on this gift. We feel the weight of conviction in our shortcomings, but the weight doesn't depress us. Instead, it moves us to ask for forgiveness and for God to change our hearts. Followers of Jesus are people who can honestly look at their faults and then allow God to change their heart!

With these two questions answered, enjoy your sleep with God close by, loving you and watching over you.

The Good Night God habit has also been called many different names, like an Examen, Nightly Review, or Review of the Day.

How Do the Daily Connections Help Unlock Life with God?

- They build our relationship with God, helping us grow in our love for Him (Key 2 Mission: Great Commandments)

- They bring God into our daily life and help us to abide in Jesus (Key 3 Motif: Abiding)

- They allow us to experience a closeness with God that

brings supernatural joy into our lives (Key 3 Motif: Enjoying)

- They are the best way to grow closer to God and let His words change our heart (Key 4 Measure: Growing)

How Often Should I Do the Daily Connections?

GOAL: DO ALL THREE PARTS OF THE DAILY CONNECTIONS AT LEAST FIVE DAYS A WEEK.

Let me remind you that it takes time to develop these habits. Sometimes it takes months. Or years. Create a reasonable plan to grow in the Daily Connections. Start small, and gradually add on. You will see God work in new ways as you do, and that's your reward! The Daily Connections will put you in God's presence each day, and as you mature you will link these three times of focused prayer with abiding prayer, taking God with you through each moment of the day. At least that's the goal, although I still have not mastered unbroken connection with God every day. I'm not sure anyone has, but the more I connect with God, the more of God's life I have in my day.

Tips for Better Daily Connections

- When you are developing the habit of the Daily Connections, it is very helpful to have a mentor who can answer questions and encourage you. In our church we have a book called *The Faith Toolkit* that is for three people to use together in practicing the Methods Key. It really helps to talk with friends about the ups and downs of adding the Daily Connections into your life.

• When you first begin the Daily Connections, often a surge of spiritual life encourages you. As you continue to practice the habit, that quick progress will become less dramatic. You'll have days where God's presence is muted, or you feel like you're not getting anything out of the time. These feelings should not discourage you from practicing the Daily Connections. Like an athlete who is training for a race, there will be good days of training and bad days. Keep training your heart. Sweet times with God are ahead, and you are showing love for Him by setting aside these times each day.

• As you become established in the Daily Connections, keep the time fresh with new options. Don't do the same thing every day for years, instead mix up what you're doing to keep things interesting. Change your verse for your Good Morning God. Read through the Bible in your Spiritual Boost time one year, then slowly read through one of the biographies of Jesus the next year. In your Good Night God, google fresh questions to help you see what pleased God and where you need to grow. There are thousands of resources to spice up your Daily Connections, so keep them fresh. Connecting with God is an amazing privilege, so work at keeping it real!

Questions to Help You Thrive

1. Which of these three Daily Connections have you tried?

2. Are you more connected to God when you read/listen to the Bible, or when you pray?

3. What can you do when you don't understand what you are reading in the Bible?

4. Which of the tips hits home for you?

5. What is your next step in building a Daily Connections habit?

Resources for a Deeper Dive

- *Hearing God*, by Dallas Willard

- *Doors into Prayer*, by Emilie Griffin

My favorite resource for Spiritual Boost help

- YouVersion Bible App Plans (free Bible reading plans and devotionals)

METHOD: WORSHIP SERVICE Δ

Nothing can set your lives straight and make them exactly right so much as can your constant attendance at church and your eager attention in listening to what is said here. What food is to the body, the teaching of God's word is to the soul.
(John Chrysostom, 4th century)

J ohn Chrysostom was a pastor from the early church, but his words could have come out of my own pastor's heart today. There is so much value to the spiritual habit of regularly attending a worship service. I have to admit, this commitment to a local community of Jesus followers was not always my priority. As a young man I felt above this "church attendance need" that others had.

Maybe it was the hypocrisy that I saw sometimes at church. Maybe it was the sermons that didn't connect with my life. Maybe it was just wanting to have Sunday mornings to sleep in. Maybe it was because at times I didn't feel like I was valued at church. Maybe it was because the evil one was, and is, always trying to divide and conquer, keeping me away from God's family and God's Word.

Then one morning in my twenties, I was reading my Bible and praying, and God spoke to me really clearly. "How can I help you grow when you are not connected to the people I have chosen to use? People in the church are My hands and feet, and you are far from My resources. It's time to join them, so you can grow faster."

So, I did. I joined the hypocrites and found out I was hypocritical in some places too. I learned to let God apply sermons when the pastor did not. I traded sleep on Sunday mornings for something better—an encounter with God and those who love Him. As I committed to my local church, I became known and recognized by the people there. I began to appreciate the gifts and insights of those in my church community. My spiritual health was better, and when a crisis came, I had new resources. I learned a lesson about being part of a church family and being a regular part of the service each week. Many other followers of Jesus have similar stories.

What is a Worship Service?

A worship service is any gathering of people that regularly includes four things: teaching from the Bible, connecting with each other, Communion (the bread and cup, which remind us of Jesus' sacrifice), and prayer and worship. In the Bible, the very first worship service had these four activities.

> *All the believers devoted themselves to the apostles' teaching, and to fellowship, and to sharing in meals (including the Lord's Supper), and to prayer.*
>
> Acts 2:42

The "apostles' teaching" from this verse is found in the Bible, and we devote ourselves to listening with open hearts to the truth that is there. The Bible is explained by a teacher, helping us hear God's voice and calling us to choose God's way. We learn to understand the Bible and to apply it to our lives through the teaching time at a worship service.

Fellowship is a word that means we connect with others who are exploring Life with God. This is what happens before and after the worship service, and often at shared meals with others. Sharing a meal can be a good setting to get to know others, so invite a new friend or family to lunch or dinner! You can even buy simple, premade food at a grocery store if you don't know how to cook and can't really afford to go out to a restaurant. Connecting at the worship service or over food is a great example of spiritual fellowship.

The Lord's Supper (also called Communion or the Eucharist) should be a regular part of gathering with other followers of Jesus. Jesus asked us to do this together to remember His great sacrifice that led to our forgiveness. Followers of Jesus understand the meaning of the bread (the body of Jesus broken for us) and the cup (the blood of Jesus poured out for us so we can be forgiven). We eat the bread and drink from a cup together as a sign of our need for Life with God.

Prayer and worship (which includes singing together) can be a powerful way to make us aware of God's presence, and this is a major part of a meaningful worship service. A Worship Leader shows us the way to come into God's presence, and the pastor speaks from God's Word. As we experience the presence of God, we join in worship together as a community, praying together, seeing God's power to heal poured out on hearts and bodies, and expressing with fresh awareness that God is worthy of our love and praise.

So **GO**, even if it's late on Saturday night or early on Sunday morning. Record that sports game and show your kids that God and God's family are a priority for a follower of Jesus. If you can't attend in person, join your church community online to stay connected. Make it a regular part of your week!

Worship services have been called by many different names in history (Mass, Divine Service, Church Service, Love Feast), but they all have these four parts described in the Bible.

How Does Attending a Worship Service Help Unlock Life with God?

- It teaches us the truth of what God wants us to do, so we can abide by obeying Him (Key 3 Motif: Abiding)

- Celebrating Communion reminds us of our need for forgiveness in our Life with God (Key 3 Motif: Being Real)

- It puts us in a group to praise and worship God, enjoying Him together (Key 3 Motif: Enjoying)

- The teacher is an example of how to grow in our relationship with God (Key 4 Measure: Growing)

- We start friendships with others as we talk before and after the service (Key 4 Measure: Caring)

How Often Should I Go to a Worship Service?

GOAL: ATTEND AT LEAST THREE WORSHIP SERVICES A
MONTH, AND VOLUNTEER TO HELP AT LEAST ONCE A MONTH.

To be part of a church family, you need to regularly connect with people, and to be part of the movement of God in your church, you need to hear what your pastor is saying. Be fully there when the Holy Spirit brings you to tears during the worship. Feel the encouragement of God to share your faith or serve others with love. Turn away from sin when the Word of God comes in conviction and you realize you've failed God. Find the restoring power of sharing a difficult situation with someone who says "Can I pray for you?" Enjoy the laughter of friends reconnecting and new acquaintances sharing coffee.

Then also volunteer once a month to help with the many ministries that happen at a weekend service. Help with the kids or babies, make a pot of coffee, serve on the Tech Team, help someone find a seat, hand out programs, or be a musician on the Worship Team. That's part of being in this faith community—lending a hand!

How Does This Affect Monique's Life with God?

A member of our church, Monique, shared her view on the weekly worship service:

"My week starts off with 'spiritual Sunday' and that sets the tone for everyone in my family. I actually feel the Holy Spirit when I'm together with God's people. It's a feeling, not just something I know in my head. Our pastors are just regular people, and when they share their struggles, I know it's OK not to be perfect.

The time we are singing worship songs is the most intense feeling of them all. It's so powerful to be singing and worshiping together. I can hear others singing—it's not just me. Then we do Communion together, and I know it might sound funny, but even hearing Pastor Theo chew makes it feel like we're all connected together with God. Then after the service there is conversation—it's light. The Holy Spirit in people—it's light. It's life. Showing up the first time was so hard, but then everyone is so beautiful. I tell people they should come because I want them to experience that beauty."

Top 5 List

I want to offer you my own recommendation by listing some important events that have happened for me in a worship service (my Top 5 list).

Here are my five top experiences from a worship service:

1. Enjoying fresh maple donuts with coffee. I feel the presence of God when I bite into a good maple donut!

2. Seeing God heal a woman with stage four cancer after we prayed for her.

3. Watching my daughter immersed in worship singing as a young adult hungry for more of God. I was so proud.

4. Having God work in my heart to forgive someone who hurt me as a child.

5. Experiencing God's presence with such vivid sensations that when I open my eyes this world seems like a shadow compared to the spiritual dimension of prayer.

That last highlight is something that I experience frequently in our worship services. It is like a recalibration of my life where the things of this world become fainter and the things of God grow brighter. It's a reset for my spiritual life, like finding true north on a compass. And sometimes I even get donuts. Did I already say that?

Tips for a Better Worship Service Experience

- The days when I don't feel like going to church are usually the days I need to be there the most. Just do it.

- Know that there is a spiritual battle to keep you away from the worship service. Expect more conflict with your family, your car to break down, or an argument with your friend from church. Don't let these stop you! Frustrate the evil one who wants to destroy your faith and keep you away from His people.

- The night before the service, read the verses that the pastor will teach on the next day. This will get your heart ready for what is taught.

- If your church community is learning a new song

together, listen to it during the week, so you can join in singing with more confidence and increased meaning.

- Invite a friend who needs encouragement to come with you to church and sit next to them. It's always fun to have a friend join you!

- During the service, don't get distracted by things. Decide that you are here to worship God, hear from Him, and enjoy the community. Our love for God and others should outweigh the temptation to get annoyed by someone's clothes, the kind of music being played, or someone who is lifting up hands in worship. Some people benefit from sitting closer to the front, so they don't have as many visual distractions.

- After the service, consider if God wants you to love someone by listening to them, praying for them, or inviting them to lunch.

- Remember the three reasons you are here: to hear from God's Word, encounter God, and enjoy warm community. Pray for these. Seek them out. The worship service is a powerful method to unlock your Life with God!

Questions to Help You Thrive

1. What are the four important parts of a worship service?

2. Which of these four parts is your favorite? Which one do you probably need to appreciate more?

3. What's a significant spiritual event that happened in a worship service for you or someone you love?

4. Which of the tips hits home for you?

5. What is your next step in building a worship service habit?

Resources for a Deeper Dive

- *The Sabbath Experiment*, by Rob Muthiah

- *Worship*, by Ron Allen and Gordon Borror

Method: Core Groups △

Once upon a time in real history "churches" were just a
few families meeting in a home to worship, learn, and
enjoy community. There were no buildings or arenas filled with
followers of Jesus. There were no world-class musicians helping
with the singing. There were no master of divinity degrees for the
leaders in these house churches. It was just the Holy Spirit leading
in their hearts, God's Word taught by simple folk, and a small
house church living life together. These early churches began to
multiply, and followers of Jesus went from about one hundred

people to over six million before church buildings were ever built in AD 325.

People who followed Jesus didn't have to join a small group, because they only met in small groups! Over and over again in the last 2,000 years, those who want to experience Life with God rediscover this basic fact: spiritual growth will be stunted and uneven unless you are part of a small group focused on exploring Life with God together. We call this group a Core Group, because it is a core part of discovering Life with God. When your core muscles are developed, lots of things get easier in life. When your Core Group habit is solid—same!

What is a Core Group?

A Core Group is a type of small group, with between six and fifteen adults. It's not a Bible study group, although the Bible is read and discussed each week. It's not a therapy group, although people share their struggles and needs, and confidentiality is important. It's not a ministry team, although the group will serve others in the community. It's not a prayer group, although people pray together at every Core Group gathering.

A Core Group is the third important habit (method) to help you thrive in your Life with God, because it is the social setting for working on all the balanced measures from Key 4: growing, caring, serving, sharing. While attending a worship service dips your toe into community, a Core Group immerses you in honest relationships that should become a spiritual family. Each Core Group has Core Group Pastors who lead the group and help you grow spiritually. This is such a helpful habit to add to your Life with God!

Here are the weekly parts of a typical Core Group, which lasts for ninety minutes:

- Opening Question: A fun question for adults or kids to answer so you get to know each other.

- Bible Discussion: Core Groups are the place to talk about the Bible, not teach the Bible. Usually, the teaching and Bible passage come from the pastor's last message at the worship service. The Core Group Pastor asks questions and the group members talk. Many people can't learn unless they talk, so these conversations are a very important part of letting the Bible sink into their lives. Core Groups emphasize applying the Bible to our lives.

- Sharing Life Updates: Each Core Group member shares the name of one person on their Sharing Life List at the beginning of each year (see Key 5: Sharing Life List). All people in the Core Group pray for the Core Group

Sharing List, asking God to bless the lives of these friends, neighbors, coworkers, and family members. Each week, Core Group members share updates on how these loved ones are doing.

- Prayer Requests and Prayer: Group members offer prayer requests from their own lives, and prayer for these needs is done to close the group time.

Here are the quarterly parts of a typical Core Group:

- One service project where members of the group meet a need of someone outside the church community. It is great if this person is on the Core Group Sharing List. Our friends and neighbors who don't yet experience Life with God are often impacted by the love shown in Core Group service projects.

- One outreach social where the group invites people on their Core Group Sharing List to have fun and get to know the people in the Core Group. When Jesus' followers gather for fun and laughter, the joy of Life with God shines! How beautiful it is to invite our coworkers and friends to experience the love and joy of God's kids at a social event.

Every Core Group has a shared mission: *The relationships and activities in Core Groups are an important part of helping believers grow in their faith. Each group will be focused on discussing and applying the Bible, building community through sharing, praying, and serving together, and reaching out through quarterly service and outreach socials. Core Groups are led by pastors who care for the members, model spiritual maturity, and challenge those in their groups to become more like Jesus.*

Core Groups are the house churches of history, but today it's hard to find one name that identifies them. Some call them Life Groups, or Missional Groups, but it's the function of the group (encourage the four measures) and the leadership (a Core Group Pastor) that distinguishes a Core Group from other small groups.

How Does Attending a Core Group Help Unlock Life with God?

- This is the only one of the five methods that is connected to **every** aspect of Life with God, so it's easy to see why we call these gatherings *Core* Groups!

- Discussing and applying the Bible helps us understand God's approach to life and allows us learn from others how to interact with God (Key 3 Motif: Abiding and Key 4 Measure: Growing)

- We build community by authentic sharing with our Core Group, and our prayers and support for each other help us find Life with God, even in difficult times (Key 3 Motif: Being Real and Key 4 Measure: Caring)

- In all these activities, we find joy in growing, caring, serving, and sharing (Key 3 Motif: Enjoying)

- We are on the lookout for needs to be met in the lives of those on our Core Group Sharing List, and we serve together once a quarter (Key 4 Measure: Serving)

- As we pray and share with those who need Jesus, we become spiritually tuned in to the work of God in the lives of these loved ones (Key 4 Measure: Sharing)

How Often Should I Go to a Core Group?

GOAL: ATTEND AT LEAST THREE CORE GROUPS A MONTH

You will experience a thrill as you get to really know the people in your Core Group. Jesus will work in your heart and give you love for these unmasked people, and you will discover that we are all in need of caring and compassion. Being consistent in a group is essential. You are an important person to the others and are missed when you don't attend. Your commitment is to attend your Core Group for one year.

How Does This Affect John's Life with God?

A member of our church, John, shared:

"Going to a Core Group during the week helps keep me connected to God through the Bible and our church community. It helps keep me more focused on God in a daily way, instead of just having Sunday morning, then dealing with the world all week long. Because of my past, spending time in a Core Group helps me to shed the anger I tend to have. I see more of the beauty that God has for me.

Instead of just trying to connect with God on my own, community helps me to do it together with others. If I'm on my own I might procrastinate and put it off, but with a group you are doing it right there! I gain a little bit from everyone's knowledge and views, and I incorporate it into my own life—like how iron sharpens iron. I miss our Core Group during the summer when we don't meet as often. I feel more disconnected from God and will be glad when we start meeting again!"

Tips for a Better Core Group Habit

- Prayerfully visit at least two different Core Groups before choosing one to be your Core Group for the year.

- During the Core Group gathering, remember that everyone needs to participate. If you have ten people present for the ninety minutes, that means your part of talking at the meeting should be about nine minutes. If you regularly take up other people's time to talk, you will need to grow in supportive listening instead of always answering.

- Groups have a natural dynamic where at first there is a lot of energy and lots of connections happening. After six months, you will typically run into the "family feel," where you are bothered by some of the habits of other group members. This is natural, and God is trying to help you rely on His love to love others well. The final stage is a real affection for others, even though you have seen them without their masks on and know their strengths and weaknesses. Don't bail out in the middle of this process. God has such good gifts to give you in a Core Group!

- Pray for your group and those on your Core Group Sharing List at least once a week in your Spiritual Boost time.

- When you are on your way to gather with your group, pray that God will use you to care for one person at the Core Group.

- Schedule something social with a person in your Core Group outside of the weekly meeting.

Questions to Help You Thrive

1. What is the difference between a Core Group and a Bible Study group?

2. Which part of a Core Group meeting sounds the most helpful to your spiritual growth right now?

3. How do you think a Core Group Pastor might help you grow more quickly?

4. Why is regular attendance at a Core Group important to

becoming a disciple of Jesus?

5. What is your next step in making the most of a weekly Core Group?

Resources for a Deeper Dive

- *Missional Small Groups,* by M. Scott Boren

- *Leading Life-Changing Small Groups*, by Bill Donahue

METHOD: SERVING HOUR Δ

> The credibility of our witness is directly tied to the compassion
> of our actions. A church that doesn't serve is a church that
> struggles to be heard. (Christine Caine, 21st century)

I have a passion to make Life with God clear and accessible to every person. As we learn about each of these methods, it's easy to feel overwhelmed. I want to remind you that God is hoping you will just take the next step. Start with the Daily Connections, then add in regular worship services. Next, make space for a weekly Core Group. Take one step at a time. Remember the map in the background of Key 5, which means you're on the route. Don't get frustrated that you're not further along the path. Just take the next step when you can. God loves you right where you are, and there is more joy ahead as you grow deeper in a thriving Life with God!

One of the shocking things Jesus said is that *He* came to serve *us*. Do you understand how strange it is that God, the Architect of the universe, the Uncaused Cause of everything that exists, the One whose thoughts become reality, this God took on human form to serve us, the created ones? No other world religion would dare to suggest such a thing for their deity. It would be embarrassing or blasphemous, or both. Jesus' way to God is different, unexpected, and turned upside down compared to our natural inclinations. He came to serve, so we should serve too!

What is the Serving Hour?

Serving is just finding a need and meeting it. This is what we do in God's family. This is what God does for us. This is what Jesus did over and over. The Serving Hour is an hour spent meeting someone's need who is outside your faith community. There should be no expectation of return. Here are some examples of Serving Hour tasks:

- Send an encouraging note to someone who is struggling

- Volunteer at a local food pantry for those who struggle to have enough to eat

- Coach a youth sports team to support healthy activities for community kids

- Donate blood

- Make cookies for a neighbor (People always have a need for cookies! Especially pastors . . .)

- Go together as a Core Group to pull weeds at the house of someone on your Core Group's Sharing List (more on this in the next chapter)

I have found that if I pray about serving others during my Spiritual Boost time, God will show me a need to meet. If you are having trouble finding a way to serve, make it a focus of prayer, and God will direct you!

How Does the Serving Hour Help Unlock Life with God?

- Serving makes God's heart happy as we reflect Jesus' compassion in our own lives (Key 2 Measure: Great Commandment to love God)

- Serving should flow from a love for others that gets nothing in return (Key 2 Measure: Great Commandment to love others)

- When someone abides in God, that person feels joy in helping those who God wants to help (Key 3 Motifs: Abiding and Enjoying)

- Having a regular goal for serving helps our intentions become a reality (Key 4 Measure: Serving)

How Often Should I Do a Serving Hour?

GOAL: DO AT LEAST ONE SERVING HOUR EACH MONTH

As you add the Serving Hour commitment into your life, a beautiful attitude will develop. You will start looking for needs in your daily life. I find myself saying, "Have I done my June Serving Hour?" For me, my next step was to schedule a regular volunteering job, and I have done that for the last five years. This way I don't ever miss a month. I worked in a food pantry for people who need help with groceries, and then in a shelter for people who have no home. Choosing something that reflects your natural joys in life can make it even easier: people, pets, kids, health support, counseling, etc.

How Does This Affect Ricky's Life with God?

A member of our church, Ricky, shared:

"When I was left to my own ways, I was depressed and relying on alcohol to fix my life. It wasn't until I accepted Jesus and I started doing service that it took me out of that and helped me to see natural gifts that I didn't know I had. When I am at the food pantry where I volunteer, I just tell God, 'I don't know who I'm here for, and all You're asking is for me to be alert. Help me stay in Your Spirit.'

I'm seeing a side of life that I hadn't seen before—people who just need the basics like food. I hope they will see God in me, like in the song that says, 'Even in just a smile, they might feel the Father's love.' Serving shows me that it doesn't matter where those people are at. Jesus is sending me where the light is needed. I love to see God using me to shine His light."

Tips for a Better Serving Hour

- Ask God to show you needs in the lives of the people outside of your immediate family and church community.

- When meeting a need, open your heart to God's presence, and tell God you are doing this out of love for Him and the person. I like the Breath Prayer (a short prayer you can say over and over), "Serving like You."

- I find that a busy schedule needs a set time to serve, so once you've found a good place to serve, make an ongoing, scheduled commitment.

- There is something refreshing about serving in an area outside of your normal focus in life. For example, if you are a professional who works with people (manager or sales), try doing something physical for your serving (pull weeds or help repair cars).

- People with certain disabilities or physical limitations may have more trouble finding a place to serve. Two opportunities that we have found where people can serve regardless of physical limitations are card writing and prayer. Here are some other possibilities: phone calls to shut-ins, English as a second language help, hospital visits, extra financial giving, and preparing or buying a meal for someone in need.

- Switching up your Serving Hour periodically can be energizing. A change puts you in contact with different challenges and new people who need Jesus.

Questions to Help You Thrive

1. What are three reasons we should serve others?

2. Why is serving the antidote to selfishness?

3. How would you discover if people around you have a place of need?

4. What kind of service is the most interesting to you?

5. What is the next step to implementing a Serving Hour in your life?

Resources for a Deeper Dive

- *Serving as Jesus Served,* by Michele Howe

- *Celebration of Discipline,* by Richard Foster ("Service" chapter)

METHOD: SHARING LIFE LIST Δ

I wish that every believer here, whether member of this church
or of any part of Christ's family, might see to it
that from this day on he or she would shine as a light
in the midst of the darkness of this world, giving light
to those that come within the range of their influence.
(Charles Spurgeon, 19th century)

Have you ever had a close relationship with a parent who has lost a child? The loss is a life-changing experience for every person I know who endured it. Some parents have lost a child to suicide. Some are lost due to a drug overdose. Some of them didn't have a child who physically died, but their son or daughter has cut off all contact with them. For them, there is a longing, an empty space that will never be completely filled. Even the most healthy of them still have a sense of longing and loss.

So, when I hear the parables (stories with a point) Jesus tells about those who don't yet follow Him, I carry that mood of longing into the stories. Jesus' stories tell us that God looks on those who have not come home into His family as lost children.[25] As we grow closer with God, we can feel more and more of His longing for people to experience Life with Him. It's not just about this lifetime, either, because there are eternal consequences to this life. God is a father who has lost a child, and soon that child may be separated from Him forever. We can help Him by being His ambassadors of love.

> *So we are Christ's ambassadors; God is making his appeal through us. We speak for Christ when we plead, "Come back to God!" For God made Christ, who never sinned, to be the offering for our sin, so that we could be made right with God through Christ.*
>
> 2 Corinthians 5:20–21

Jesus has done the hardest work by opening the way to God through His death in our place. Now that the door is open, God invites those He loves (everyone!) to enter through the door. Jesus has secured our release from the prison of our selfishness and mistakes, and now God urges us to come home—to come home and experience Life with God. To return to the way things were in the garden of Eden when He walked and talked with Adam and

Eve each evening. To become the people He intended when He made us.

This is the story He wants us to tell others. Our story. Jesus' story. Life with God begins with a miracle. I hope your heart is thrilled at the possibility that God might use you to help bring one of His lost children home!

What is the Sharing Life List?

The fifth and last method to help us love like Jesus is about turning the desire to be ambassadors for God into a reality. Remember, these methods are all about putting practical plans into place, so people can practice what they preach (I'm pretty sure seven *p*-words in a sentence makes it perfect. So . . . you're welcome!). A nice copy of this card is in the back of this book in a section called "Extra Stuff: Key Card."

Sharing Life List

Ask God to highlight 2 local loved ones who need Jesus. Consider neighbors, coworkers, co-volunteers, friends, and family.

---------------------   ---------------------

Core Group Sharing List

---------------------   ---------------------

---------------------   ---------------------

---------------------   ---------------------

---------------------   ---------------------

Pray | invest | invite

Pray   for God's blessing on them
invest time in caring for them
invite them to a CCC event

B ody – physical needs
L abor – work/school needs
E motional – heart needs
S ocial – relational needs
S piritual – spiritual needs

Prayer is the oxygen of Life with God and abiding in Jesus. We want to start with praying for the lost people in our life, because that's where we unlock God's power in their life. That's where we unlock God's power in *our* life. We want to do more than wish for them to experience God's blessing; we want to pray for it! We want to have a concrete plan, and we want God's Spirit guiding us at each step. So, our Sharing Life List starts with a focus on prayer.

I'm going to ask you to pray about the names you put on your Sharing Life List. Ask God to use you to love someone who is local and needs Jesus. I keep a copy of this card in the Bible I use for my Spiritual Boost time each day, and then I pray once a week for each person on the card. I encourage you to write their names on your card.

Then, you're going to invest and invite those people. You're going to pray for them at least once a week, you are going to invest in caring for them and bringing good things into their lives, and you are going to invite them to an event at your church that fits them.

You might invite them to a Trunk or Treat event. You might invite them to a walk with the women's group. You might invite them to a Giants' baseball game with a men's group. You might invite them to a worship service, because you think, "Oh, they're going to love this topic—we're talking about how to raise your kids." Pray for God to give you direction on what event your loved one might attend. Remember that as God's kids, His own Spirit is in in you and can guide you.

How Do I Pray for My Friends on the Sharing Life List?

Ask God to bless the people on your Sharing Life List, using the word **BLESS** to remember all the ways they can thrive.

B is for body, reminding you to pray for any physical needs that they have. Have they started a new workout regimen? Are they on a diet? Is there some health struggle in their life? Pray for God to give them success in those places.

L stands for labor, meaning whatever they're doing for their work or their school or whatever they spend time doing outside of taking care of themselves. Ask God to help them thrive at their work.

E is the emotional side of their life. What's happening emotionally in their life? Are they anxious? Tired as a parent of young children? Prone to depression? Ask for God to fill them up and help them find joy.

S is the social part of their life, such as what's happening in their family or in their friendships. Every one of us has some relationships that are difficult, so we pray for God to help them be patient and wise with difficult people.

S means spiritual needs. Pray that their eyes would be opened to the truth, and that they would hunger for more, for Life with God. Ask God to give them an understanding of His great love.

How Do I Listen to God About What I Should Do Next?

After you pray for them in this way, just sit quietly and listen for what God brings into your mind (this is an example of listening prayer). In that place, that sacred place of prayer, when you've just prayed for this person that you love, listen to God. What does God want you to do? What ideas come to mind about how you can invest in them? What needs do they have that you could meet? Don't just focus on the spiritual dimension in their lives—love them as a whole person like God does.

Sometimes, when I'm listening, I hear God urge me to talk to them about something specific in their life—perhaps a question or an encouraging word. I will say, "OK, Father," and then the next time I'm talking with them, I bring it up. It's a very abiding way of sharing and caring about people. We share what God is doing in our lives with them, and then invite them to come to something at our church.

When we share what the Holy Spirit puts on our hearts during prayer, then He can grab onto those words as we speak them.

He whispers in them, "Hey, this is the truth. You know how I've been tugging on your heart. Did you hear what that person said? They're telling you something that is from God!" All of a sudden that person has a God-moment where it's not just you talking, but it's God speaking through you, and they feel it. And that's amazing for both you and your friend!

You can also see there is a place for adding the names of one person for each member of your Core Group. All the group members offer one person's name to add to their Core Group Sharing List, and all people in the Core Group pray for these people to be **BLESS**ed as well. Prayer unlocks the power and blessing of God in the life of your Core Group's loved ones.

How Does Using a Sharing Life List Help Unlock Life with God?

- It brings God great joy to have one of His lost children come home, which brings us joy because we love Him (Key 2 Mission: Great Commandments)

- It engages us in Jesus' mission to help others find Life with God (Key 2 Mission: Great Commission)

- It brings great joy to see God work through us to help a loved one find Life with God (Key 3 Motif: Enjoying)

- It's a practical way to be sure we are loving like Jesus by sharing our faith with others (Key 4 Measure: Sharing)

How Often Should I Use my Sharing Life List?

GOAL: PRAY THROUGH YOUR SHARING LIFE LIST
ONE OR MORE TIMES A WEEK

Be sure to write down what God nudges you to do or say to the person on your card. This is another reason a journal is helpful for your Spiritual Boost time. Sometimes what God is calling you to do or say is a little bit uncomfortable, but you should trust our Father. He knows the power of what He is asking you to do or say. The possible benefits for your loved one are too many to count, so a little discomfort is not a reason to ignore God's call to you. Pray, invest, and invite!

Tips for Using Your Sharing Life List

- I find that picking a day of the week to pray through my Sharing Life List is best, so choose a day, and make it a habit to pray during your Spiritual Boost on that day.

- Sharing about what God is doing in our lives is something the evil one tries to stop us from doing. Since he can't hurt God directly, he wants to hurt those God loves, entangling them in addictions and selfishness, souring their marriages, and poisoning their families. So, there will be resistance—a spiritual battle—as we speak the name of Jesus to others. That's why we pray *before* connecting with our friends, open our hearts to abiding in Jesus *during* our time together, and ask the Holy Spirit to use our actions and words *afterward*. Don't be discouraged if you don't see any fruit when you pray, invest, and invite! Keep loving and following God's leading.

- It can be a good thing to tell your friend that you are praying for them each week, and to ask what you can pray for. This will make them aware of the power of prayer. For example, your friend might be looking for a new job, and might suggest that you pray for them to find a job. As they see God opening up doors, they experience God's love through your prayers.

- I like to think about what I want to share from my own Life with God before I see them. If I'm going to connect with a person on my Sharing Life List, I usually take some time during my Spiritual Boost to think about how God is working in my life, so I'm prepared when it fits into our conversation.

- I don't usually share the "big life events" with others but the little things that show how God is always active in my life. Here's an example: "This week I was feeling down and had a meeting with a brother in Jesus that was filled with honesty and a desperation for God's leading. We talked and then prayed together, and it was as if a weight had lifted from my heart. I felt the presence and power of God as we prayed, and left feeling encouraged and filled with faith." These short little stories of God's work are the kinds of things I try to share with those who need Jesus.

- Remember the Key 3 motif of "being real." When you are sharing with another person about spiritual things, don't try to become the Bible Answer Scholar who answers every question even when you don't really know the answer. When someone asks a question you haven't thought about, just say you don't know! Often intellectual questions from others are not the real issue. You can assure them of one thing: God is changing your life for the better. It's better to be honest than brilliant anyway!

SUM (KEY 5 METHODS)

Methods are the foundational habits that make our Life with God a reality.

The **Daily Connections** are Good Morning God, the Spiritual Boost, and the Good Night Review (Goal: At least five days a week)

The **Worship Service** is a weekly time of worship, prayer, communion, and teaching on the Bible (Goal: At least three times a month, volunteer once a month)

The **Core Group** is a small group that meets to help grow in all four aspects of a disciple—growing, caring, serving, sharing (Goal: At least three times a month)

The **Serving Hour** is a commitment to meeting needs outside of your church community (Goal: one hour each month)

The **Sharing Life List** is a tool to help you pray and share with people who need Jesus (Goal: pray each week and follow God's leading to invest and invite others)

Like the other Keys, these methods are summed up in a nice graphic in the "Extra Stuff: Key Card" section.

Questions to Help You Thrive

1. What does it mean that God considers every person a "lost

child" until they believe in Jesus?

2. How might using the Sharing Life List help you focus on helping others find Life with God?

3. Of the three actions on the card (pray, invest, invite), which is the hardest for you to do regularly?

4. Does it sound exciting to be used by God to help another person find Him?

5. What is your next step in using the Sharing Life List with two people in your life?

Resources for a Deeper Dive

- *The Six Conversations,* by Heather Holleman

- *B.L.E.S.S.,* by Dave Ferguson and Jon Ferguson

Wrap Up

Unlocking Life with God

G ood job making it through the book to this final chapter! Or good job skipping all those chapters and reading the ending first! I see you people who read the ending of the book, you Revelation-lovers (the ending to THE book, the Bible!).

So, let's just go over this once more to be really clear. In the picture above, you see the 5 Keys, and I wonder if you picked up on the visual hint that each of these graphics has a hidden *M* in the key cuts to remind you that all the keywords start with *M*. Just a little easter egg for the nerds in our midst.

Key 1: A Miracle

The place it all starts, Key 1, is a miracle. If you are trying to follow Jesus without the Holy Spirit's help, I have good news! It's much easier with God's help. It's much lighter with God's forgiveness. There's much less anxiety with God's peace. Start by choosing Jesus as your Rescuer and Leader (Savior and Lord), following the path Jesus opened up for everyone by His sacrifice, His forgiveness, and His Spirit in you! You will have eternity with God that all His kids look forward to, and that is a hope that holds us in the storms of this life.

Key 2: Our Missions

Next, Jesus provides us with Key 2, our missions. He gives us two "great" missions: the Great Commandments and the Great Commission. The Great Commandments reveal that love is at the heart of God in a special way, and that loving God, others, and ourselves is the best way to sum up what it means to have Life with God. Like some old hippie wearing a frayed tie-dye shirt, God is all about love. Unlike that hippie, God combines love and power and deep wisdom. God's love is loyal and deep, and we can never be separated from it in this life.

The second mission that Jesus highlights is the Great Commission. We are on a "CO-mission," a mission shared with God. It is a mission to tell others how to find Life with God. Part of loving others is sharing our Life with God with them. With God in the lead, we love in deeds and are ready to share the keys to Life with God.

Key 3: Life Motifs

Motifs are themes, so here we remember three tracks of background music that should constantly play in our hearts. If someone asked the question "What is notable about <your name>?", we hope that these three motifs would come up. We hope that each of us would be an example of these motifs in our daily life at home, work, and play. I remember these motifs with the phrase "You **ARE,**" where each letter in **ARE** is a reminder of the motif.

You are **Abiding**, staying connected to God through the Holy Spirit. As much as we can, we are aware of God's presence, praying for spiritual resources in whatever we are doing, and obeying God's guidance and commands as much as we can. When we can't, there is repentance and forgiveness. This place of trust, of God-awareness, of connection through the Holy Spirit in us, makes Life with God rich and powerful and life-changing.

You are **Being Real**, honest with others about what happens in your life. A religious mask is just as offensive as any other mask, and because of God's love and forgiveness, we can transparently share what is good and not good in our lives. We bring everything we can into the light, and with trusted people and God we hold back nothing. By being authentic, we can be healed, helped, and hopeful.

You are **Enjoying**, feeling joy as you go through your day. Much of this joy is from our connection to God, who is perfectly good and loving and gives us an eternal feeling of hope. We can praise Him even in the darkest valley of this life. The soundtrack of *Enjoying* also comes from recognizing that God gives us good gifts. We can appreciate the blessings of a good friend, the way God provides for our basic needs, and the beauty of an alpine lake or our favorite singer.

Maybe someday your friends will say, "She has this connection with God that gives her peace. And she's not faking it—she's the real deal—she tells it like it is. She always brings such good energy wherever she is. She has been through some hard things, but she feels the good things even more." That is a rich Life with God!

Key 4: Measures of Jesus' Kind of Love

Jesus calls us to follow Him, keeping a balance among the four aspects of love. These are the four measures of our spiritual maturity, which are the four ingredients of Jesus' love. When all four are present, our lives spin along with the power of God, and we are filled with love and do eternal things with God each day of our lives.

Growing: We can grow in our love for God each day (how cool is that!). Even Jesus grew closer to God as he matured.[26] Our relationship with God is the most important thing in our life, so we should get to know Him and increasingly feel close to Him like we do any other close friend or mentor.

Caring: We are part of a family of God, and we need to learn to love and be part of the bigger family of God's kids. This means committing to a local church and building relationships with people who are exploring Life with God like us.

Serving: Just as Jesus came to serve others, so we meet needs. Not just the needs of other followers of Jesus, but also to those outside our church community. We learn to serve with no expectation of return, just as Jesus did, and we find real joy in the giving.

Sharing: Another way that we practically love and bless those around us is to share our Life with God with them. We don't exaggerate to make God look good. We just tell people what God is doing in our lives. For those we love who need Jesus, we share our greatest treasure with them, because it can transform their life in the same way, making an eternal difference.

Key 5: Methods to Make it Practical

Now we move to what we should DO. Our previous four Keys cover what we should be (child of God), what we should aim for (Great Commandments and Great Commission), what should be the themes of our life (abiding, being real, enjoying), and what four measures balance our love (growing, caring, serving, sharing). Now we make it practical, possible, and powerful! To grow, just start with the first method that you are not doing currently, and begin to add it to your life. Pray, ask God for help, and slowly implement these methods. Our Father will be so pleased!

Daily Connections: At least five days each week, let these three special moments with God anchor your day: Good Morning God, a Spiritual Boost, and Good Night Review.

Worship Service: At least three times a month, attend the same worship service and start making friends with the people who also attend there regularly. Volunteer to help out once a month at the service to support what God is doing in your church community.

Core Group: At least three times a month, attend a Core Group that is focused on Life with God and encouraging each other to be growing, caring, serving, sharing followers of Jesus.

Serving Hour: Once a month, meet a need of someone outside your church community.

Sharing Life List: Once a week, pray for two people on your Sharing Life List. Spend time listening to God's direction after asking Him for help, and then invest in those people with your time, inviting them to a relevant church event when it comes up.

Doing all five of these methods should take about seven hours a week, which is a significant commitment. The return on your investment (ROI), though, will be life-changing. Jesus lived to *show* us Life with God and died to *make a way to* Life with God, and now we have this treasure of Life with God. These seven hours each week are a small way to say "Thank you, Jesus!" As is always true with God, you will get far more than you give and He will be pleased by your effort to walk with Him.

Prayer for You

Let me just pray for you before I wrap up the time we've shared together in this little book.

Δ Δ Δ Δ Δ Δ Δ Δ Δ Δ Δ Δ Δ Δ Δ Δ

Our Father, I stand alongside this dear one right now
and bring them into Your presence. We stand before
You with a strange confidence, because we have no
hope in ourselves alone. The strange part is we have
never-ending hope, because You are with us, You are
for us, and You are in us. You are working through us
to do good in this world.

We want more of You in our lives—more love and
joy and peace and power. Now, as this dear one has
taken the time to read these thoughts, bless them.
Show them that You are a gentle Leader who will
rejoice in their progress. Show them that You don't
want them to do it alone, but instead want them to
open their lives to Your constant presence, and to
explore Life with God surrounded by other followers
of Jesus. Bring mentors and friends for their spiritual
journey, and draw them closer and closer to You and
the thriving life You want for them.

Protect this dear one from the enemy who brings
confusion and doubts and discouragement. Encircle
them with Your truth and love and help them
recognize that dark voice in their mind as the evil one.
In the name of Jesus, I claim this dear one for Life

with God—full life, a life You created for them, a life
of meaning and community and eternal significance
and joy.

Now, I ask You to guide them in a specific step
forward—not because of guilt or compulsion, but
because they long for more of You. They wish to
love those around them more. They want to see
themselves in Your eyes as Your child. So, give them
a path to thrive with You alongside them always. In
the name of Jesus, Amen.

Δ   Δ   Δ   Δ   Δ   Δ   Δ   Δ   Δ   Δ   Δ   Δ   Δ   Δ   Δ   Δ

Extra Stuff: SWORD Bible Study

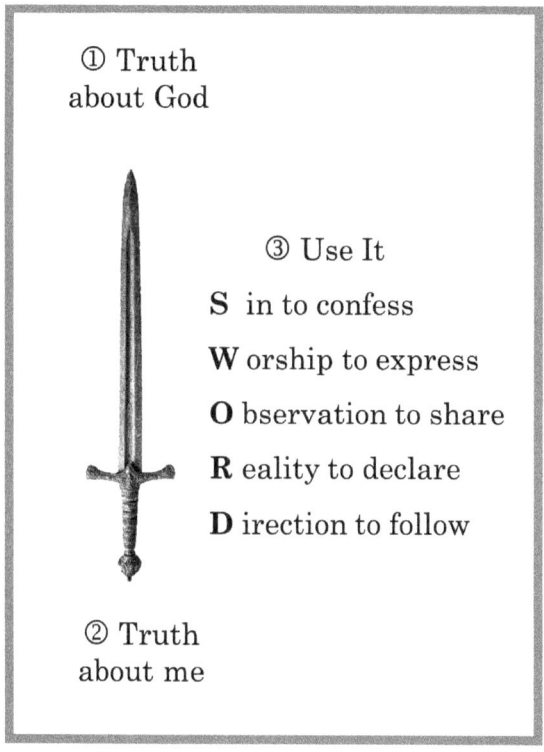

① Truth about God

③ Use It

S in to confess

W orship to express

O bservation to share

R eality to declare

D irection to follow

② Truth about me

The SWORD method is a tool that helps you apply what you are reading in the Bible. God refers to His Words as a sword that fights the lies in our lives and leaves the truth. It's like a scalpel used by a skillful surgeon to cut out the cancer and leave the healthy parts.

For the word of God is alive and powerful. It is sharper than the sharpest two-edged sword, cutting between soul and spirit, between joint and marrow. It exposes our innermost thoughts and desires.

Hebrews 4:12

How Do I Use the SWORD Method?

After reading a passage that moves us, we ask three questions:

1. What can I learn about God in these verses?

2. What can I learn about people in these verses?

3. How can I apply and use these truths in my life?

When it comes to applying the verses to my life, the third question, I use the letters of the word SWORD to help me think through different ways to apply it. You might spot just one, or maybe you'll find more. There's no pressure to find all of these. You are simply listening for what God brings to your mind.

Sin to Confess – something that I need to ask God to forgive and help me overcome

Worship to Express – something that makes me want to praise God in prayer or song

Observations to Share – something I can share with a person in my life

Reality to Declare – some self-talk I need to repeat to myself to remind me of what is true

Direction to Follow – something I want to do or do better with God's help

An Example

This morning I read John 20:3–9. After reading it, I realized that the reason that the "other disciple" believed was because the graveclothes of Jesus were left in the tomb. They knew Jesus' body was not moved, because His graveclothes were neatly folded in the place where the body was laid. This little detail helped them believe.

So, let's think about our three questions one at a time.

What can I learn about God? I think He leaves clues like the pile of graveclothes for us. We never HAVE to believe, but there are enough clues to allow faith to blossom.

What can I learn about people? In these verses, there are two disciples, but only one believes after seeing the empty tomb. The same facts can lead one to faith while one still doubts.

How can I use this in my life? Direction to Follow—when I pray for people on my Sharing Life List, I will specifically pray that God give them faith to believe!

Extra Stuff: Key Card

This card for your Bible summarizes the methods we talked about. You could just tear out the page, or copy it, or take a pic.

5 Key Methods to Life with God

Daily Connections
5+ times a week

Worship Service
3+ times a month

Core Group
3+ times a month

Serving Hour
1+ times a month

Sharing Life List
Pray 1+ times a week
Invest & Invite regularly

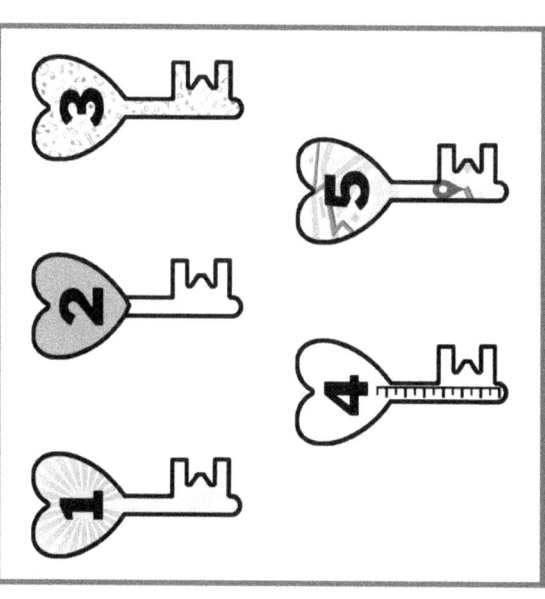

5 Keys to Life with God

Sharing Life List

Pray | invest | invite

Pray for God's blessing on them

invest time in caring for them

invite them to a CCC event

B ody – physical needs

L abor – work/school needs

E motional – heart needs

S ocial – relational needs

S piritual – spiritual needs

Ask God to highlight 2 local loved ones who need Jesus. Consider neighbors, coworkers, co-volunteers, friends, and family.

Core Group Sharing List

ENDNOTES

1. I want to know Christ and experience the mighty power that raised him from the dead. I want to suffer with him, sharing in his death, so that one way or another I will experience the resurrection from the dead! (Philippians 3:10–11)

2. *The Journal of John Wesley,* by John Wesley

3. Charles Wesley's hymn "Amazing Love"

4. He is so rich in kindness and grace that he purchased our freedom with the blood of His Son and forgave our sins. (Ephesians 1:7)

5. God sent him [Jesus] to buy freedom for us who were slaves to the law, so that He could adopt us as His very own children. (Galatians 4:5)

6. And because we are His children, God has sent the Spirit of His Son into our hearts, prompting us to call out, "Abba, Father." (Galatians 4:6)

7. But the person who is joined to the Lord is one spirit with him. (1 Corinthians 6:17)

8. For the Lord is the Spirit, and wherever the Spirit of the Lord is, there is freedom. . . . And the Lord—who is the Spirit—makes us more and more like him as we are changed into his glorious image. (2 Corinthians 3:17–18)

9. And this is what God has testified: He has given us eternal life, and this life is in His Son. Whoever has the Son has life; whoever does not have God's Son does not have life. (1 John 5:11–12)

10. We love each other because He loved us first. (1 John 4:19)

11. If someone says, "I love God," but hates a fellow believer, that person is a liar; for if we don't love people we can see, how can we love God, whom we cannot see? And he has given us this command: Those who love God must also love their fellow believers. (1 John 4:20–21)

12. Jesus said, "Your love for one another will prove to the world that you are My disciples." (John 13:35)

13. The complete story is in Luke 15:11–32.

14. They will be punished with eternal destruction, forever separated from the Lord and from his glorious power. (2 Thessalonians 1:9)

15. But the Holy Spirit produces this kind of fruit in our lives: love, joy, peace, patience, kindness, goodness, faithfulness, gentleness, and self-control. (Galatians 5:22–23)

16. We know how much God loves us, and we have put our trust in His love. God is love, and all who live [abide] in love live in God, and God lives [abides] in them. (1 John 4:16)

17. If we love our brothers and sisters who are believers, it proves that we have passed from death to life. But a person who has no love is still dead [abides in death]. (1 John 3:14)

18. The Bible's words about Jesus were originally written about 2,000 years ago in the ancient Greek language. We have many great translations of this part of the Bible into modern English, but my personal favorite is the New Living Translation (NLT). You will notice that in the Bible verses listed in this book, the actual word *abide* never occurs. The translators thought the word *abide* was too old-timey. When the NLT translates the Greek word μενω, it uses the words *remain* or *lives with*, or something like that. The translation that I believe conveys the meaning of the Greek word in today's language is *stay connected.*

19. Each time he said, "My grace is all you need. My power works best in weakness." So now I am glad to boast about my weaknesses, so that the power of Christ can work through me. That's why I take pleasure in my weaknesses, and in the insults, hardships, persecutions, and troubles that I suffer for Christ. For when I am weak, then I am strong. (2 Corinthians 12:9–10)

20. *Letters by a Modern Mystic,* by Frank C. Laubach

21. Dear brothers and sisters, I close my letter with these last words: Be joyful. Grow to maturity. Encourage each other. Live in harmony and peace. Then the God of love and peace will be with you. (2 Corinthians 13:11)

22. https://www.thegospelcoalition.org/article/reflections-on-50th-anniversary-of-my-diving-accident/

23. Never stop praying. (1 Thessalonians 5:17)

24. The words of Jesus about this are in Matthew 25:31–46.

25. See Luke 15:11–32.

26. Jesus grew in wisdom and in stature and in favor with God and all the people. (Luke 2:52)

About the Author

Theo Myer is a spiritual explorer who found the One, Jesus, after much searching. He is really grateful to be surrounded by a good group of people who know him deeply and still love him. He has a strange educational path, with degrees in education, psychology, theoretical mathematics, and biblical studies. Somehow these various educational excursions fit perfectly into God's path for him, and Theo is currently serving Jesus as a pastor at Corralitos Community Church in California.

Theo enjoys reading, watching the Golden State Warriors, hiking and mountain climbing (especially in Yosemite!), and maple donuts. His passion, though, is to make Life with God accessible to everyone and to walk beside people who are finding Life with God (and to eat maple donuts with them!). His ministry partner and true love, Gayleen, is also his wife (wife and work wife rolled into one). He has three adult children (Jordan, Sierra, and Hunter) and a couple of young people so loved they are family (Aidan and Parker). These are all super impressive people, and Theo seems much cooler when in their company.

Thank you for taking the time to consider my thoughts, and I hope you find God speaking to you through some of them.